CHORAL ARRANGING

for

SCHOOLS, GLEE CLUBS and PUBLICATION

A complete guide for the problems of choral arranging for all types of voice
combinations and for all kinds of choral groups in schools,
churches, communities, or professional organizations.

by

HARRY ROBERT WILSON

Professor of Music Education
Teachers College, Columbia University

PRICE $4.00 in U.S.A.

Copyright 1949

ROBBINS MUSIC CORPORATION
799 SEVENTH AVENUE · NEW YORK

ACKNOWLEDGMENTS

The author is gratefully indebted to all of the publishers who have kindly permitted him to quote excerpts from their publications, namely: Leo Feist, Inc., New York; Miller Music Corporation, New York; Hall and McCreary Co., Chicago; Clayton F. Summy Co., Chicago; Silver Burdett Co., New York; C. C. Birchard and Co., Boston; Carl Fischer, Inc., New York; G. Schirmer, Inc., New York; Paull-Pioneer Music Corp., New York; Associated Music Publishers, Inc., New York; Galaxy Music Corp., New York; Shawnee Press, Inc., New York; Theodore Presser Co., Philadelphia; Augsburg Publishing House, Minneapolis.

Dedicated
To all my students who have submitted
numerous manuscripts to me for examination.

TABLE OF CONTENTS

CHAPTER I

THE GIST OF CHORAL ARRANGING

The phenomenal growth of the number of amateur choruses and glee clubs during the past twenty years has opened a new field of music writing; and, has turned both the composer and publisher to developing suitable materials to meet the demands of these groups. Since choral organizations are of such varied types and represent many degrees of technical proficiency, the publication of suitable material which will fill the need of every situation becomes increasingly difficult.

Therefore, many choral directors are forced into the necessity of arranging and composing suitable choral numbers for their own individual groups. Also, publishers are turning more and more to arrangers and composers having direct contact with the choral field for compositions which will be suitable for the greater number of choral organizations in schools, churches, and communities.

FOR WHOM THE BOOK IS DESIGNED

Practically nothing has been written which can be used as a guide in writing choral numbers for these amateur groups. Consequently, the creative efforts by amateurs in the field are often clumsy and lack professional artistry, even though they contain good basic choral effects. On the other hand, many professional arrangers fail to realize the limited vocal and technical facility of these groups. They are not familiar with the devices which will obtain the maximum effects without the necessity of elaborate means. Moreover, in response to the increasing demand, many schools are introducing courses in choral composition and arranging, and including many assignments in choral writing in their general harmony courses. Students need a fundamental guide for this work.

This book is an attempt to provide useful principles and devices in choral arranging for amateur choruses of all types and degrees of development. It is addressed to the professional arranger, the amateur who wishes to perfect his creative efforts, and for the student in his growth as a musician and composer.

WHAT THE BOOK IS ABOUT

In the writing of this book it has been assumed that the reader has a basic understanding of the principles of harmony and counterpoint. Without this understanding, musical ideas are bound to appear nebulous and ineffective, if not actually disconcerting when produced on paper. However, the common pitfalls of chord connection, doubling and distribution of parts, and basic devices of good counterpoint will be indicated in the various musical examples.

Only the actual problems of choral arranging will be discussed in this book. *What is choral arranging?* It has to do with every aspect of choral writing except the creation of the original musical idea (which is the realm of musical composition). The arranger must be creative even though he deals with a previously conceived musical idea, which he may change so that it bears little resemblance to the original. Different parts of the same composition may represent both original writing and arranging, such as Brahms' "Academic Overture" or Bach's treatment of well-known chorales in his cantatas.

The arranger with his imagination and technical facility may transport a mediocre musical idea into an effective choral piece. The composer of choral music must not only have superior musical ideas, but also the imagination and technical skill of the arranger if his music is to sound as though it were intended for human voices. The sources of musical ideas are as unfathomable as the depths of the sea but the basic principles of arranging can be learned and put into practice.

SCOPE OF CHORAL MUSIC

Musicians have indulged in many a lively debate about the relative values of orchestral and choral music. The extended means of technical facility, variety of tone color, as well as the pitch and dynamic range possibilities of the orchestra have caused most of the great composers to turn to it for some of their most prodigious musical ideas. Nevertheless, the masters have also turned to the art of choral and vocal writing to express many of their most intimate and sacred emotions, as found in the works of Bach, Mozart, Schubert, Brahms, and Wagner. Moreover, the English, French, and Italian composers have a glorious choral tradition. The Russians have written some of their greatest music for the church. Our American composers are also discovering that instruments, with all their technical advantages, cannot replace the human voice for the expression of many of their most poignant musical feelings.

Choral music must be conceived in terms of the technical and emotional qualities of the human voice. This unique quality is best observed in the style of writing called *a cappella** which is the modern label applied to all unaccompanied singing. There may be an instrumental accompaniment which should enhance the vocal expression. However, sad to relate, when an orchestral accompaniment is used, it often becomes, at least in performance, the tail that wags the proverbial dog.

There are many different combinations of voices which can be used in a complete composition, or, the combinations may be shifted within an individual number to attain musical and tonal variety. The scope of choral music depends upon the technical and emotional scope of the human voice. Any emotion that can be expressed by the voice, which practically includes the entire gamut of human emotion, can be expressed in choral music. The choral composer or arranger has the added advantage of the use of words with their suggested meanings and emotional connotations to support tonal ideas. There is also the possibility of using voices in the manner (not imitation) of instruments for tonal and rhythmical effects, such as humming, neutral vowel sounds and use of consonants. These effects must be used judiciously and in keeping with the general character of the composition or arrangement. They should tend to make the word text more effective or to create mood, and not become an end in themselves.

---

*NOTE SPELLING

MATERIALS FOR CHORAL TREATMENT

For the choral composer practically any text from the Bible, lyric poetry or suitable prose can be used as a possible vehicle for a musical composition. Even the laundry list has been the source of inspiration to composers in their so-called lighter moments. However, the arranger must turn to existing melodies and texts for musical treatment.

The source of this material which offers the greatest opportunity for creative imagination is the *folk song*. It tends to lend itself to the most effective choral writing, partly, at least, from the fact that it originally sprang from the sorrows, joys, and labors of the people themselves. There are many sources for these songs: the singers of folk songs, editions of folk songs, (be careful of copyrights) and a collection at the Library of Congress in Washington, D. C. This rich source of material is available to any arranger who is free to spend the time examining it. There is still an untapped wealth of folk songs from all lands, especially those of the Latin-American countries, which will make stunning choral arrangements.

The *modern song* of the master composers is another source of material for the arranger. Extreme care and judgment must be exercised in the selection of songs that are to be given choral treatment. Care must also be taken to retain the harmonic texture and musical flavor of the original. Songs with simple melodic line and harmonic structure are the ones which usually can be developed into the best choral arrangements.

There is always the adverse argument that, if the composer had intended his songs for choral singing, he would have arranged them himself. Anyone acquainted with the intimate ways in which composers work will know that this is not necessarily the case. Also, there are many examples where composers have given their own melodies, as well as melodies of others, various kinds of musical treatment.

However, arrangers today should approach the master songs, as well as the lesser songs of Stephen Foster and other writers, with respect and care in their effort to present them in a medium where they may be more widely used. There is opportunity for real musical service here.

The *popular song* of the day usually lends itself to choral treatment of different combinations of voices. This is due to the fact that the melodies are usually not complicated and the harmonic structure is straight forward. When arranging these numbers the harmonic structure should follow, to a considerable degree, the vogue of the day. Rhythmic effects should predominate. Often, the arrangements of these songs are too difficult to warrant the amount of rehearsal time necessary for amateur groups to master them. One should not attempt to "dress them up" entirely out of keeping with the simplicity of the original song, at least, not for amateur groups.

Novel and rhythmic effects are the key to success in arranging these songs. The flavor of the professional arrangements of these songs can be attained with modest harmonic and rhythmical means. Then, amateur groups will enjoy rehearsing them and can prepare them for performance in a short time.

The *arranging of instrumental numbers* for choral groups is a questionable procedure. This objection is not necessarily based on the fact that, since the composer did not originally conceive them for voices, they should remain unmolested. A choral arranger has as much right to arrange instrumental compositions as choral numbers as the instrumental arranger has in taking folk songs, art songs, or popular songs and making instrumental numbers out of them. However, it just so happens that most instrumental melodies do not lend themselves to the addition of a text for a satisfying musical result. The melodies are usually difficult or ungracious for singers when words are added to them. It is for this reason, rather than because they are sacrosanct, that choral arrangers should be cautious and careful in using them.

Certain instrumental numbers, such as the choral section in "Finlandia" by Sibelius and portions of "Les Preludes" by Liszt, seem appropriate to use with words. But these are few and far between and, unless the instrumental number (either piano, violin, or orchestra) has natural choral qualities, it had better be left alone in its original form.

The same objection does not hold true for the *re-arranging of standard choral numbers* for different voice combinations. Granted that it is best for the music to be done in its original form, still, if the voices are not available to sing it, a different version is acceptable. Many composers wrote with specific groups in mind for example, Handel when he composed "The Messiah" for the resources of the Dublin Choral Society. Otherwise, they might have written differently or for another combination of voices.

Some of the old masterpieces for mixed voices sound well when arranged for treble or male voices. If not made available for these voices, then many girls' and boys' glee clubs in this country would be denied familiarity with much beautiful music and suitable material. Many of the songs written by Brahms for treble voices would sound well for SATB. Quite a number of the modern choral compositions and arrangements today are published simultaneously for mixed, treble, and male voices.

CONCLUSION

Remember that, in choral writing the complicated musical treatment is not always the most effective. Choral writing must be more lucid and transparent than orchestral writing. Therefore, look for simple but appealing melodies, texts that offer varied rhythmical and vocal treatment, and songs that invite a contrapuntal line for development of interesting voice parts.

CHAPTER II

CHORAL RESOURCES

The voice, with all of its technical limitations, is the most expressive of all single instruments. Of course, that statement is a platitude but in essence it is true. Of all the instruments the voice can produce the widest variety of tone color and also numerous sound effects. Some readers may cite the pipe organ to refute this statement but the pipe organ is a combination of many instruments.

The voice is the only instrument to use vowels and consonants to pronounce words. This factor not only gives literal meaning to musical ideas, but also, it affords infinite subtleties of tone color. The choral arranger must understand and explore the tonal possibilities of the human voice if he is to write for it effectively.

TYPES OF VOICES

Voices are classified in accordance with their individual quality and range possibilities. The choral arranger need not concern himself with the former, but rather, with the *normal* tone quality of each *general* division and its range and dynamic possibilities. It may be of interest, however, to point out the types of voices which usually sing a given part. There is no universal practice in assigning voices to parts, largely on account of the difficulty of classifying untrained voices.

Soprano I (1st soprano)
{
Coloratura, (brilliant, very high range)
Lyric, (pure, velvet quality, high range)
Dramatic, (full, resonant, range usually to high Bb)
}

Soprano II (2nd soprano)
{
Lyric, (those singers whose range is not too high)
Dramatic, (those voices often too heavy for Soprano I)
Mezzo-soprano, (full, resonant, approaches contralto quality with medium high range)
}

Alto I (1st alto)	Mezzo-soprano, (especially useful on this part for high notes) Lyric contralto, (full, velvet quality with low notes)
Alto II (2nd alto)	Contralto, (full, resonant, sombre, extreme low notes)
Tenor I (1st tenor)	Lyric, (pure, ringing, high range) Dramatic, (full, resonant, used only on this part when high notes are easy and free)
Tenor II (2nd tenor)	Lyric, (when high notes have not been developed) Dramatic, (when high notes are strained or voice is too heavy for 1st tenor)
Bass I (1st bass)	Baritone, (warm, colorful, wide range)
Bass II (2nd bass)	Baritone, (when high notes have not been developed or when rich low notes are in the range) Bass-baritone, (rich, firm low notes) Basso, (contra-bass notes possible)

RANGE OF VOICES

Although the chorus does not have the extended pitch range of the orchestra, due to the physical limitations of the voice, its range is sufficiently wide to offer a wealth of contrast to the arranger. Individual voices of the same type may vary by as much as an octave. However, there is a normal range for each voice part, which the arranger can use without hazarding objections on the part of choral directors.

The pitch ranges indicated below are for adults and students of senior high school and college age. When writing for very young voices of the elementary and junior high school age, it is necessary for the arranger to observe further limitations in the practical ranges of various parts. The degree of these limitations will be pointed out in Chapters V, VI, and VII.

In the following charts, the white notes "o" indicate the range which we are assured is within the range of most amateur choruses who have received adequate vocal training from their directors. The black notes "●" are possible with well-trained groups but they must be used with discretion.

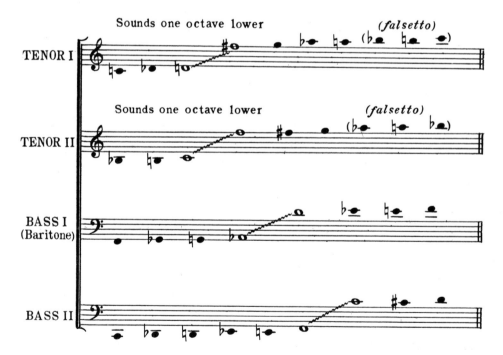

Use extreme low notes only for contrabass parts that are doubled one octave higher.

An aggregate of the normal individual voice parts over a grand staff gives the arranger the following pitch resources.

TESSITURA

The extreme ranges of voice parts may often be used if these extremes are not sustained over too many notes or too long a time. *Tessitura* means the general highness or lowness of a song or voice part. If a part stays in the upper half of its range for a period of time, without any relief by skipping to lower notes, it is said to have a high tessitura; a part that remains in the lower half of the voice range is said to have a low tessitura. Very often it is not the high or low note, but rather the general tessitura, that causes difficulty for amateur voices. This is especially true of the part that has a high tessitura, because the strain is taxing for inexperienced singers. Their voices tire until after a while they are unable to reach the notes without undue strain, if at all.

These musical examples show voice parts with extreme tessituras.

Ex. 1

CHORAL SYMPHONY
LAST MOVEMENT

SOPRANO
Allegro assai

van BEETHOVEN

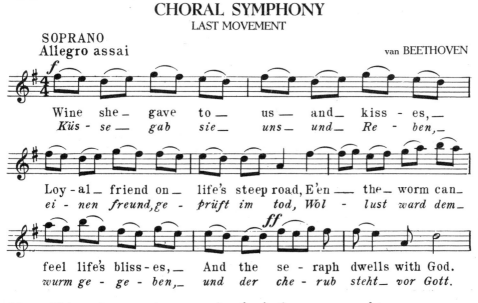

Note: This entire score is very taxing for both sopranos and tenors.

In the music of the Russian church, such as the following example, effective use is made of a contra-bass part. Although the extreme low notes may be sung an octave higher, much of the sonority is lost when this is done. The ending is also quite low for sopranos, but since the part is written in unison with the altos who are singing in a comfortable range, the sonority is not impaired.

Ex. 2

LET THY HOLY PRESENCE
(S.S.A.T.T.B.B.)

P. TSCHESNOKOFF
Arr. by Noble Cain

Sometimes singers are unable to reach extreme high or low notes preferred by the arranger. In these cases, optional notes (other harmonic notes) are written for the parts where these extreme pitches occur.

Ex. 3

IN STILLY NIGHT

J. BRAHMS
Arr. by H. R. W.

SOPRANO

The fall-ing dew in sil-v'ry hue,

ALTO

The fall-ing dew in sil-v'ry hue,

BARITONE

(1) Choral Program Series, Book IV. Silver Burdett Co., New York.   Used by Permission.

TEMPTATION

Lyric by
ARTHUR FREED

(T. T. B. B.)

Melody by
NACIO HERB BROWN
Arr. by H.R.W.

TENOR I

If you were will-ing, — If it can nev-er be, Pit-y me

TENOR II

If you were will-ing, — If it can nev-er be, Pit-y me

BASS I

If you were will-ing, — If it can nev-er be, Pit-y me

BASS II

If you were will-ing, — If it can nev-er be, Pit-y me

★) High notes may be sung by a few selected voices.

DYNAMIC LIMITATIONS OF VOICES

Although well-trained voices have a wide range of dynamics (from *pp* to *ff*), the amateur and young voice usually does not have sufficient control to obtain much contrast between loudness and softness of tone. Practically any choir with proper direction can quickly learn to sing a lovely soft tone but they cannot sing a rousing *forte* without evidences of strain. With proper vocal training the chorus can learn this control but the singing of thrilling *forte* passages are not evident in most of the amateur and school choruses.

Therefore, the arranger must accept to some degree this dynamic limitation and prepare his climaxes accordingly. It is well not to sustain *forte* passages for too long a time without some relief, and great care must be taken to write piano and orchestral accompaniments so that they don't completely cover or "drown out" the singers.

MUSICIANSHIP OF SINGERS

The ability of singers to read music fluently is notably bad. Most choirs learn their music by the rote process or by "picking out each part." Schools and the directors of amateur choruses are taking steps to correct this general weakness but not much success is evident.

Therefore, arrangers must be careful not to write intricate parts when simpler ones will get the effect and do just as well. When complicated harmonic difficulties arise, a passage in unison may be the solution. Canonic treatment is easy to learn and often offers an interesting way out of difficult spots. If complicated parts are written they should be, as in the great compositions of Bach, worthy of the rehearsal time necessary to master them.

CHAPTER III

BASIC TECHNICAL CONSIDERATIONS

Although this book is written on the premise that the reader has acquainted himself with the rules of harmonic and melodic writing, some observations and cautions will be pointed out to correct the most obvious faults usually found in amateur arrangements. These suggestions are not presented as rules because the secret of choral writing is inherent in the music and the choral effects desired. However, before an arranger can feel free enough to experiment with novel effects, he must first be thoroughly familiar with the standard harmonic effects which will be illustrated in this chapter.

HOW TO BEGIN

In arranging a song, it is quite a good idea to block it out (plan it) completely before beginning the details of writing. The usual procedure is to let the melody stand out in relief at the beginning before resorting to changes of key, mode, and rhythmical effects for variety. Then, a return (or a suggestion of a return) is usually advisable before the end to give a feeling of three-part form. Folk songs often lend themselves to this treatment. For the same reason, it is often best to begin a song, especially a popular one, with the chorus, then to the verse, returning to the chorus for the ending. In arranging an art song the form or structure is largely determined by the music as it stands.

One does not necessarily start an arrangement at the beginning and continue on to the end. He may start arranging with the body of the song, or, with some special cadence or middle section into which he wishes to develop the arrangement. Introductions and codas are often written after the body of the arrangement is finished, just as the preface or introductory chapter of a book is often written last.

INTRODUCTIONS OR PRELUDES

What the arrangement should begin with is often a problem. Four or eight measures of piano accompaniment, drawn from the body of the composition, are often used before the voices are introduced. A novel introduction using piano and voices is often effective in setting the mood of a piece. The following example shows the development of a choral introduction from the piano introduction of a popular song. It is written for male voices.

Ex. 5

from the Musical Play "Rio Rita"
THE RANGERS' SONG
(WE'RE ALL PALS TOGETHER)

Lyric by
JOSEPH McCARTHY

Music by
HARRY TIERNEY

Ex. 6

from the Musical Play "Rio Rita"
THE RANGERS' SONG
(WE'RE ALL PALS TOGETHER)
Glee Club T.T.B.B.

Lyric by
JOSEPH McCARTHY

Music by
HARRY TIERNEY
Arr. by H. R. W.

The following novel introduction utilizes sound effects in the basic rhythmic pattern of the song.

Ex. 7

CINDY*
(S.A.T.B.)

TRADITIONAL
Adapted by H. R. W.

MOUNTAIN DANCE SONG
Arr. by H. R. W.

The use of humming or neutral vowels is very effective for introductions to set the mood for quiet numbers.

Ex. 8

OFT IN THE STILLY NIGHT
(S.S.A. a cappella)

IRISH AIR
Arr. by H. R. W.

Ex. 9

POOR WAYFARING STRANGER

WHITE SPIRITUAL
Arr. by H. R. W.

From "Poor Wayfaring Stranger" octavo 2528

DISTRIBUTION OF PARTS

Successful arranging depends largely upon writing tuneful vocal lines in compact harmony. To do this, the arranger must be melody-conscious but still not lose the solidity of close harmony. Soprano and alto should stay within an octave as a rule. The same is true for alto and tenor. It is occasionally permissible for tenor and bass to be wider apart than an octave but not for too long a time. Although the following examples are for single chords and do not necessarily represent the distribution of voices in contrapuntal vocal writing, they still remain the basis for compact harmonic writing.

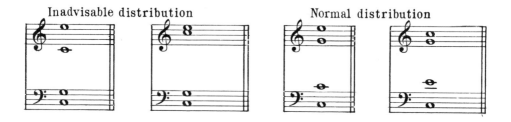

Occasionally, an arranger may disregard the above distribution of parts but only to retain the melodic line of a voice part, or, to secure a unique choral effect. See also Ex. 25 written for treble voices.

Ex. 10

MARY HYMES
(S.A.T.B.)

JAMES STEPHENS   SAMUEL BARBER

she _____ is a rune, she is a rune,

is a rune, she is a rune, she is a rune, she is a rune,

__ is a rune, __ she is a rune, she is a rune,

rune, is a rune, she is a rune, she is a rune, she is a rune,

DOUBLING OF PARTS

The usual rules for harmonic writing as to the doubling of parts should be rigidly observed in choral arranging. These rules may be relinquished when writing in contrapuntal style, where the melodic line of the voice part is paramount; or, where some special choral effect is desired.

Briefly, these rules are:

1. Do not double the third of the principle chords of a key (I, IV, V).

Questionable   Satisfactory

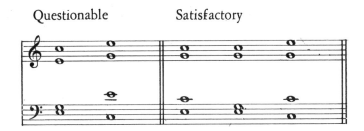

2. It is usually best to double the third of the secondary chords of a key (ii, iii, vi). Think of these chords as substitutes for IV, V, I in this order and treat them accordingly.

Satisfactory   Permissible   Questionable
                      (More minor effect)

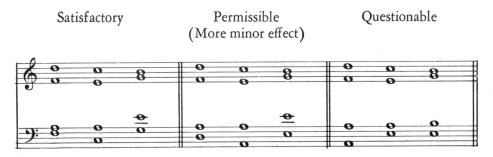

3. As normal practice, do not double the leading tone of a key.

Questionable   Advisable

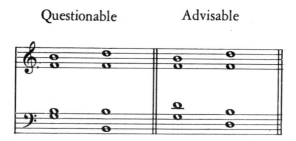

4. Dominant Sevenths. It is standard practice to omit the fifth of the dominant seventh chord and double the root when the chord is in fundamental position. In the inverted position, it is best to include all four tones. Today, much more freedom is being exercised in the resolution of these chords. Normally, the seventh of the chord always moved down but now it is used freely in either direction, especially when some other note moves to the note to which the seventh would resolve.

Satisfactory   Normal resolutions   Permissible resolutions

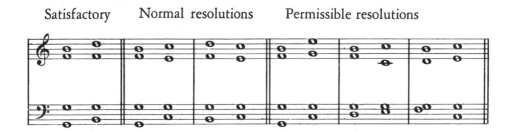

CHORD CONNECTION

Likewise, basic harmonic principles in chord connection should be followed unless relinquished in the use of sequence, contrapuntal line, or special tonal effects.

1. *Parallel Fifths and Octaves*

These bugaboos of the harmony student should be avoided, not so much because they sound badly to the modern ear, but because they destroy independence of parts, a necessary factor in fine choral arrangements. Naturally, octaves appear in unison passages, and fifths, if treated as in the example below, are effective.

Ex. 11

ALLELUIA
CHORUS FOR MIXED VOICES

H. R. WILSON

★ Two accompanists at one piano are needed.

This composition takes advantage of the possible antiphonal effects between treble and male voices. Unusual rhythmic effects may be secured by following closely the accent marks on different syllables of the word "Alleluia." Sing as fast as it is comfortable for the singers to maintain rhythmic accompaniment.

If only a few tenors are available they may all sing first tenor part.

2. *Nearest Chord Progression*

The old rule of the common tone and moving the other tones as nearly stepwise as possible holds good. The shifting of the melody prevents the retention of the common tone at times but, if so, the other voices should generally move to the nearest chord tones. Wide skips, especially in the inner voices, should be avoided. Overlapping of voices should only be used for special effect. Within the limits of harmonic principles, each part should be made as melodically interesting as possible. This means that there should be no hesitancy to dispense with rules if the parts are harmonically sound and singable.

3. *Harmony Over the Bar Line*

Since the music progresses to a stressed beat over the bar line it is usually best to change the harmony. The same harmony over the bar line is weak and tends to give a monotonous effect.

4. *Difficult Skips*

All parts should be written in accordance with sound melodic principles. After wide skips, it is best to reverse direction unless the melody represents some chord. Do not skip after a stepwise run, as a rule, especially over the bar line. As mentioned above, be careful of wide skips in inner parts; they are usually difficult to sing. Avoid the augmented second and the augmented fourth intervals, especially in inner parts. Most important of all, avoid a descending skip of the seventh in the bass. Work out the passage so the skip down can be an octave. Then the basses will have no trouble since they handle skips of a fifth and octave easily.

SHIFTING OF THE MELODY

It is common practice for the sopranos to carry the melody. As a result, the inner parts often become a succession of repeated notes or otherwise very uninteresting melodically. To give the singers, as well as the listeners, more variety, it is wise to shift the melody between different parts. This practice should not be abused by trying to shift the melody every few notes. The change should usually be maintained for at least the length of a four measure phrase, if not longer.

CROSSING OF PARTS

At times, it may seem unavoidable to cross parts if interesting melodic lines are to be secured. This is often the case with inner parts (alto and tenor). However, it is a fact that any choral arrangement which has much crossing of parts is difficult and confusing to the average amateur singer. It is wise for the arranger to make adjustments so that the parts will not need to cross.

Especially is it unwise, in mixed-voice writing, to take the alto above the soprano and the tenor below the bass. It would be better to shift the melody to a different part before the necessity of crossing these parts arises.

In writing for male voices, since the harmonic spacing is so close, it is often necessary to cross parts, such as writing the second tenor above the first tenor and the interchange of baritone and second tenor parts. However, crossing of parts in male voice arrangements can be kept to a minimum by the judicious selection of keys and the careful shifting of melody at opportune times. Again, however, the arranger is cautioned not to shift the melody just with occasional notes, but for a considerable length of time, at least a musical phrase.

USE OF RESTS

An amateur arrangement can often be detected by the lack of imagination in the use of rests. The loveliest part of the music may be the rests. Don't continue all parts without any interruption. Permit one part to rest and bring it in later, perhaps in canonic treatment. This should not only be done to give the singers a rest, but also, for the musical effect. Dramatic pauses should be utilized in all parts. Make a study of the effective ways in which composers use rests.

CLOSING CADENCES

An arranger should be familiar with the effect of closing cadences. In fact, he should plan the type of cadence that he wishes to use in various sections of the piece and work toward them. He should acquaint himself thoroughly with the sound of the usual cadences as the following:

Preparatory		Cadence	
VI II^6} 1$^6_4$		V^7	I
VI } III } IV		V^7	I
I^6 } VI } II^6		V^7	I
VI } II } IV		I	

These cadences are common. There are many other possibilities but the arranger must first be at home with these. Notice that the final chord is never used in fundamental position to prepare a cadence. Save it for the end so that it will sound fresh.

At the end of sections or the close of the piece, the arranger should study the effect of rising and falling cadences; the first gives the feeling of excitement or a majestic quality while the latter gives a feeling of repose. The entire character of an ending can be determined by the decision to take the bass up or down.

CLARITY OF WORDS

In vocal music words are paramount. They give precision and mood to the performance. Therefore, in arranging choral music the words must not be so covered by the music that they cannot be understood. The value of counterpoint and rhythmical shifts to make the parts more interesting are questionable if the use of these devices obscure the text, especially where the text is subtle or necessary to the full meaning of the music. Many arrangers resort to humming or a neutral vowel in the harmonic parts instead of the shifting of words to avoid covering the text. This is a moot point with arrangers, however.

CODAS

Just as with introductions, many arrangements seem to need a short ending of some kind beyond the body of the arrangement to give it a feeling of finality;

and also, to make it more attractive in performance. Sometimes this ending may be a replica of the introduction with a different cadence. It may grow out of a deceptive cadence, or it may have an individual character of its own. Compare the following coda with the introduction of the same arrangement in Ex. 7.

Ex. 12

CINDY*
(S.A.T.B.)

TRADITIONAL
Adapted by H. R. W.

MOUNTAIN DANCE SONG
Arr. by H. R. W.

CHAPTER IV

MODERN CHORAL DEVICES

As long as music is written, composers and arrangers will be seeking new ways of expressing themselves. They will continue to experiment with different types of tonal-rhythmic patterns to obtain novel and unusual effects. However, there are no short cuts to mastery of the printed score and it is essential that the novice arranger be familiar with the practices of his predecessors before striking out for himself into unfamiliar and unknown tonal paths. Any creative art is built on experience and no one should seriously try to arrange choral music in a style with which he has had practically no association.

This statement does not mean, however, that an arranger should be satisfied with just the style of writing in which composers of the past have expressed themselves. He should seek different and novel ways continuously and incorporate them into his style as fast as he can master new techniques. This chapter is designed to give some hints to the neophyte arranger seeking more modern patterns of writing.

USE OF MODES

The old Ecclesiastical modes offer to the modern ear fresh combinations which have been partly lost during the past two centuries through almost complete adherence to our common major and harmonic minor scales. A thorough study of these modes are available in many harmony text books. The arranger can quickly get the spirit of them if he will play usual chord progressions using different white notes on the piano as key or tonal centers without employing any accidentals as in the following examples.

Ex. 13   Using only white notes with "D" as tonal center.

Using only white notes with "A" as tonal center.

These progressions give a very strong minor feeling, due largely to the use of the lowered seventh step at the cadence. To offset this quality in the majority of the modes, the early contrapuntal writers often made use of the raised seventh step as in the Ionian mode (which is the same as our major scale). They employed this mixed form of the modes along with the so-called pure form. Carrying this practice a little further, unusual effects can be obtained by alternating between major and minor chords in the normal progressions of one triad to another as in the following example.

Ex. 14

*MODERN CHORDS

Not only may the classic triads be used in fresh combinations and progressions but, in the present century, much experimentation has been carried on by composers in the construction of new chords.

1. Triads with added notes.

The most obvious of these chords is simply the addition of a note, usually the sixth, to a triad. This addition forms a secondary seventh chord without the restriction of the normal resolutions of these chords. Arrangers of popular songs have utilized this system to such a degree that it has almost become banal procedure. The following example shows the harmonic effect of these chords.

Ex. 15

2. Ninth, eleventh, and thirteenth chords.

With the expanded use of ninth, eleventh, and thirteenth chords in instrumental music, a natural development led to the distribution of the notes so that the chords were built on fourths. Only in polyvocal writing do we find chords of the eleventh and thirteenth in choral music and due to the intricacies of intonation they are used infrequently by most arrangers. The following composition makes excellent use of these luscious chords, however, in fine musical taste.

*Anyone wishing a succinct presentation of the newer trends in chord building and harmonic progressions should study, "New Harmonic Devices," H. A. Miller, Oliver Ditson Co., Philadelphia, Penna.

Ex. 16

EVERY WIND THAT BLOWS
FOR CHORUS OF MIXED VOICES
(UNACCOMPANIED)

Poem by
EUGENE PILLOT
By permission

Music by
LEIGHTON LUCAS

3. Chord building on fourths.

Chords built on fourths produce an effect which is very useful when introduced occasionally. The effect becomes too bizarre in choral writing when used for an extended passage. The following examples give some hint of the possibilities.

Ex. 17   Ex. 18

4. NEAPOLITAN TRIADS

The conception of the Neapolitan triad has been extended to include, not only the one for the tonic chord, but also, each chord of a key may have its own Neapolitan triad. The examples show the various Neapolitan chords of the key of C; a resolution of the Neapolitan triad of the tonic chord; and a typical resolution of one of the other Neapolitan chords of this key.

Ex. 19

Neapolitan triads of the Key of C.

Ex. 20

Ex. 21

5. Augmented sixth chords.

The use of augmented sixth chords has also been greatly expanded. The following examples show the usual augmented sixth chords and their traditional resolutions, as well as some of the newer combinations of augmented sixth chords. In fact, if the augmented sixth interval is preserved the inner voices may be shifted around almost at will.

Ex. 22

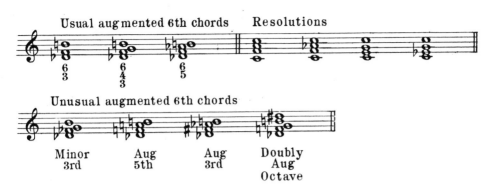

Usual augmented 6th chords   Resolutions

Unusual augmented 6th chords

Minor 3rd   Aug 5th   Aug 3rd   Doubly Aug Octave

6. Whole-tone chords.

Closely associated with the augmented sixth chords are the almost inexhaustible combination of chords which can be derived from the whole-tone scales. Since there are twelve notes in the chromatic octave there can be only two of these scales. The notes of each scale can be combined into chords at will. Use of these chords in choral music is limited but they can often be introduced for striking or bizarre effects.

Ex. 23   SCALE I   SCALE II

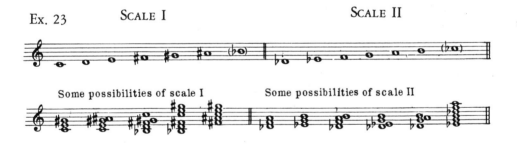

Some possibilities of scale I   Some possibilities of scale II

MODERN PROGRESSIONS

The expansion of harmonic possibilities in piano and orchestral music has opened new vistas in harmonic progressions for the choral composer and arranger.

1. Modern resolution of chords.

One of the most striking changes in harmonic progressions has been the freeing of the rules in the resolution of dissonances. The prepared suspensions of an earlier period became independent notes of the chord itself. More complicated harmonies resulted and more choices in their resolutions followed. In fact, in instrumental music, practically any combination of notes may be used as a chord, especially if their resolution is chromatic or the voice leading smooth. In choral music the arranger must continually ask himself if these ultra-modern progressions are consistent with the idiom used throughout his arrangement; and also, if the progressions are singable by amateurs. The following examples give some idea of the possibilities.

Ex. 24

The use of the diminished octave in the following manner has a special piquant effect.

Ex. 25

LITTLE LAMB, WHO MADE THEE

WILLIAM BLAKE   HARRY ROBERT WILSON

From Choral Program Series, Book II,
Silver Burdett Co., New York   Used by permission

2.   Parallel movement of chords.

A very effective choral practice, if not maintained for too long a time, is the parallel movement of the chords in a phrase. The parallel fifths in the bass of example 11 are common practice now. Also, open parallel fifths without the third of the chord have the flavor of olden times as well as a modern touch of the unusual. These liberties with fifths do not excuse the occasional and clumsy parallel fifths sometimes found in arrangements of traditional, classic harmony. These parallel fifths are due to errors in voice-leading, rather than intentional design. The following example shows the effect of parallel fifths and octaves in a sweep.

Ex. 26

ODE TO SOLITUDE

CHARLOTTE CAIN   NOBLE CAIN

Parallel movements need not be limited to fifths and octaves but may be used with any type of chord construction. Here are some whole-tone chords in fan shape, parallel movement.

Ex. 27

3. The Pyramid.

Building up to a full chord, part by part, is often used for special effect, usually at the beginning or end. However, it may be used in the body of the composition and more than one voice may be introduced at a time. Also, the chord may be built upward or downward.

Ex. 28

LITTLE DAVID, PLAY ON YO' HARP

CHORUS FOR MIXED VOICES, A CAPPELLA
(S.S.A.A.T.T.B.B.)

NEGRO SPIRITUAL
Arr. by H. R. W.

From ''Little David, Play on Yo' Harp'', octavo No. 1066
Copyright 1940 Hall & McCreary Co., Chicago   Used by permission

CONTRAPUNTAL AND CANONIC DEVICES

Since the contrapuntal style of writing is melodic it is especially gracious for choral arranging. The parts are more interesting for singers and also, usually more singable than parts conceived at the piano or those which resemble the instrumental style of writing. In arranging folk songs it is well to arrange at least one verse in contrapuntal style for variety. Also, the shifting of the melody to various parts, as suggested in the previous chapter, and writing contrapuntal lines for the other parts often gives added attractiveness to the arrangement. At the same time, this practice seems to retain the flavor of the simplicity of the original song rather than when it is accompanied with over-rich harmonies.

The counterpoint of today is usually much freer than the strict variety of the sixteenth and seventeenth centuries and it generally has a sound harmonic basis. But the practice of thinking parts melodically is a sound one for the choral arranger.

The arranging of, at least, some of the verses of a folk song in contrapuntal style gives opportunity for bridging verses and consequently, the feeling of continuity. This bridging is accomplished by having one part drop out and rest before the end of one verse, then entering before the part which is carrying the melody finishes that verse.

Ex. 29

WASSAIL SONG

42

The choral arranger must be continually on the lookout for passages which can be written in canonic style, either at the unison, the octave, or some other interval. They are easy to sing and effective in performance.

Ex. 30

THE BELLS OF ST. MICHAEL'S TOWER

WM. KNYVETT
Arr. by R. P. Stewart

From Choral Program Series Book V. Silver Burdett Co. New York   Used by permission

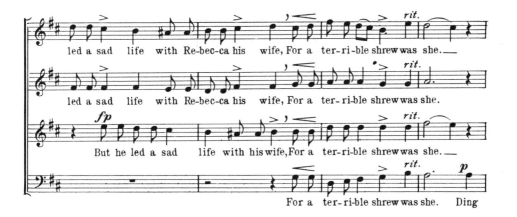

RHYTHMIC EFFECTS

The modern arranger must study the various rhythmical devices which are effective. One of these devices is in the style of chanting a phrase while one of the parts carries the melody. It is beautifully done in the following excerpt.

Ex. 31

LOST IN THE NIGHT
(MIXED VOICES)

F. MELIUS CHRISTENSEN

Another rhythmic effect that is often used by arrangers is writing the harmonic parts as a choral accompaniment for the melody.

Ex. 32

LI'L LIZA JANE
(T.T.B.B.)

De LACHAU
Arr. by H. R. W.

Also, rhythmical effects may be employed by means of vocal sounds, clapping, or percussive instruments.

Ex. 33

SKIP TO MY LOU
(S.A.T.B.)

American Dance Tune
Arr. by H. R. W.

★)CALLER: Swing your partners all around, Right foot up and left foot down,
Swing your opposite across the hall, You haven't swung her since last fall,

Make that big foot jar the ground, Now promenade your honey 'round.
Now trot home and swing your own, And thank your stars the bird ain't flown.

★) Create an atmosphere of the old square dance. All eyes should be turned toward pianist. This section may be repeated as often as desired and solos on violin, harmonica, or jews'-harp may be introduced. If stage permits, a short dance can be performed by a group of eight in front of chorus. Different calls can be used.

HUMMING EFFECTS

The modern arranger often employs humming as an accompaniment for a solo, for rhythmical sound effects as suggested above, or, in quiet passages for the tonal loveliness of humming voices. The use of humming can be overdone and the arranger should be sure that it is an integral part of the total effect desired. Humming is most effective in *a cappella* work, where it serves as an accompaniment. It is ineffective when used with piano accompaniment unless the piano part is interwoven around the humming. With organ or orchestral accompaniment, humming is practically useless because it is covered up by the sustained harmony of the instruments.

Ex. 34

THOSE HOURS WITH YOU
(S.S.A.)

H. R. WILSON

NEUTRAL VOWEL EFFECTS

As suggested in the previous chapter, choral arrangers often use a neutral vowel in some parts to supply a harmonic accompaniment for the melody. This procedure is gradually replacing the older practice of shifting words and deleting part of the text in harmonic parts, because the singing of words in these parts often covers the complete text of the soloist or the part singing the melody.

Ex. 35

from the Musical Play "Rio Rita"
THE RANGERS' SONG
(WE'RE ALL PALS TOGETHER)
Glee Club T.T.B.B.

Lyric by
JOSEPH McCARTHY

Music by
HARRY TIERNEY

Arr by H. R.W.

Neutral vowels may also be used in providing a rhythmical accompaniment, producing striking sound effects, or for tonal effects where words seem unnecessary.

Ex. 36

SIBONEY
(Glee Club T.T.B.B.)

English Words by
DOLLY MORSE

Spanish Lyric and Music by
ERNESTO LECUONA
Arr. by H. R. W.

THE DESCANT

In the early contrapuntal writing a florid melody, called a *descant* (singing against) often accompanied the more simple *cantus firmus*. In modern writing the descant is more like a countermelody based on the harmony. However, it should retain some of its florid character and is most effective when it is an independent melodic line and does not duplicate other parts. It is generally sung on a neutral vowel, although words drawn from the text may be used.

General rules for writing descants:

1. Make the descant an independent part.

2. Don't duplicate other parts unless it is absolutely necessary.

3. Enter at an advantageous point, usually where the other parts are sustaining a long note.

4. Sustained notes are good when parts are moving.

5. Figuration is good when parts are sustained.

6. The descant can be used to fill in the missing harmonic notes in the parts.

7. Some crossing of the descant with the soprano part is permitted just so long as it does not lose its own individual identity.

8. The top range of the treble voices may be extended somewhat in writing a descant but the *tessitura* must not lie extremely high for too long a time.

Ex. 37 a

SILENT NIGHT

JOSEPH MOHR

FRANZ GRUBER
Descant by Harry R. Wilson

Descant from "Songs We Sing"
Copyright 1940 Hall & McCreary Co., Chicago   Used by permission

Ex. 37 b

O COME, O COME, EMMANUEL

GREGORIAN MELODY
Descant by Charles Ripper

DESCANT (sing: *ah*)

Re-joice! Re-joice! Em-man - u - el shall come to thee, O Is - ra-el!

From Twice 55 Green Book, C. C. Birchard & Co., Boston — *Used by permission*

Ex. 37 c

AMERICA, THE BEAUTIFUL

KATHERINE LEE BATES
DESCANT

SAMUEL WARD
Descant by Harry R. Wilson

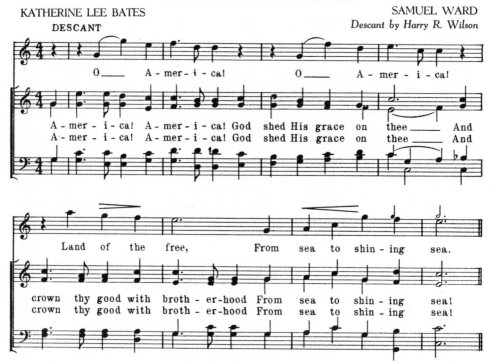

O___ A-mer - i - ca! O___ A - mer - i - ca!

A - mer - i - ca! A - mer - i - ca! God shed His grace on thee ___ And
A - mer - i - ca! A - mer - i - ca! God shed His grace on thee ___ And

Land of the free, From sea to shin - ing sea.

crown thy good with broth - er-hood From sea to shin - ing sea!
crown thy good with broth - er-hood From sea to shin - ing sea!

From "Songs We Sing" Hall McCreary Co., Chicago, Used by permission

THE SOLO VOICE

In early choral writing little use was made of the solo voice, probably due to the fact that there were usually only one or two voices on a part anyway. With the advent of larger choirs and a more harmonic style of writing, the need of solos to secure more variety in choral compositions became recognized. When a solo is used it may either be sung unaccompanied, with an accompaniment of voice parts; with instrumental accompaniment; or with a combination of instrumental and choral accompaniment. In arranging popular or folk songs for several voices it is usually wise to have one verse or, at least, a section of a verse written for a solo voice. However, the solo may be marked "optional" or "for a few selected voices" in case the choir does not have an adequate soloist. (See Ex. 32.)

USE OF SPEECH

With modern poetry there are passages which seem to defy musical settings. Therefore, some composers of choral music are resorting to declamatory passages in choral speech. This is very likely, however, a practice growing out of the desire for newer and more novel expression of creative ideas. At times, it is effective but it can be overdone and thus border on the theatrical. The choral arranger is free to use this device but he should be careful that when he does it is a natural outgrowth of the musical expression.

SUMMARY

In this chapter an effort has been made to point out some of the newer procedures and devices which the modern choral arranger can consider in his search for adequate means to express his musical ideas. Many of these newer trends are an outgrowth of the amazing development in instrumental composition. Therefore, they are not always equally successful in their adaptation to choral writing. It is well to remember that, with the technical limitations of the average amateur chorus, it is wise to avoid extravagant harmonic and contrapuntal means when simpler ones will express the music just as well.

CHAPTER V

CHORUS OF MIXED VOICES

Mixed choruses are those consisting of treble voices, (female or unchanged male) and changed male voices. The voice parts are labelled: soprano, alto, tenor, and bass. Each part is often divided into two sections (I and II). The number of singers on each part varies with different choirs, the ideal condition being when there is about an equal number on each part. However, the fact, as regards the greater number of mixed choruses is: sopranos are predominant in most groups, altos are usually too weak, tenors are just plain scarce, and basses usually manage to hold their own.

The arranger must consider the foregoing fact when assigning the melody and other important musical phrases to various parts. Nevertheless, balance of voice parts is the director's job and the arranger should not disregard the principles of good writing and produce a badly balanced score when writing for an unbalanced choir.

In arranging for the mixed chorus it is usual practice to use a separate staff for each voice part and the piano. Only one voice staff is usually necessary where a voice part is divided into two sections. However, if the entire composition (or a long section of it) is written *divisi* (divided parts) and the writing is so contrapuntal that words fall on different beats, it is best to use a separate staff for each section. The usual layout for mixed chorus score is as follows:

Ex. 38

Sometimes, to save space in an arrangement in straight harmonic style, the voice parts are condensed on two staves plus piano accompaniment. If the accompaniment is just a duplication of voice parts, it is often omitted altogether. This latter layout is found in all hymn books.

Ex. 39

As will be seen by these examples the old soprano, alto, and tenor clefs

are not used. **SOPRANO ALTO TENOR** middle C middle C middle C In modern notation the

G clef middle C is used for soprano, alto, and tenor parts with the tenor sounding one octave lower than it reads. The F clef middle C is used for the bass part at all times; also the tenor part when scored in hymn style (see above). Then the tenor sounds the actual note that it reads. So the "poor" tenors must learn two clefs.

SATB COMBINATION

The combination most usually found in mixed choruses is that consisting of SATB (soprano, alto, tenor, bass). This is the combination used in most church, high school and college choirs. There are many fine examples of music for this combination written by the great composers which every arranger should study and analyze. The principles presented in the preceding chapters must be carefully observed in writing for this combination. The arranger must give constant attention to compactness in the spacing of parts, the range of voice parts, doubling of parts and the writing of parts that are melodically interesting. He should observe caution in the crossing of parts and shifting of the melody between parts.

Even in four-part writing for mixed voices there are times when it is necessary to divide parts for a few chords to express complete harmony. Sometimes division of parts can be avoided by careful voice leading before the necessity arises. When there is a need to divide parts, it is best to divide the soprano and bass parts, rather than the alto and tenor, because there is usually a shortage of altos and tenors in school and church choirs.

SAB COMBINATION

This shortage of tenors in the high school choirs (and almost the total lack of them in the junior high schools) has given rise to another type of mixed chorus, composed of soprano, alto, and bass parts. Since the range of the bass part must be limited, it is often labelled as baritone, although this classification is usually given to a *type* of voice, rather than a voice part.

The staves used are the same as those for SATB with the omission of the tenor part. They are presented here with the advisable range for each part. Notice that the voice ranges are reduced considerably from those given in Chapter II, due to the fact that this combination usually occurs in young choirs where the voices, especially those of the boys, are not developed.

Ex. 40

White notes indicate practical ranges.
Black notes are possible, but not advisable.

In writing for this combination, care should be taken to write specifically for the SAB combination, rather than writing for an SATB combination and just omitting the tenor. Here, more movement of the alto and bass parts is necessary than in the four-part combination in order to obtain complete harmony with little or no doubling of parts. Since, in this way, the arranger is obliged to write more melodic parts, writing for this combination is good practice for him.

The bass part should be treated as a fundamental part, rather than as a tenor part with the piano supplying the bass, unless the music calls for this effect. Naturally, the root of the chord in the bass will result in an incomplete chord at the cadence if the melody also ends on the root of the chord. The alto, then, must end on the third unless the open fifth ending is desired. The normal progression of the alto, in some instances, does not lead easily to the third of the chord at the cadence. When such is the case the arranger may write the regular tenor part in small notes at the cadences, with instructions for a few basses to sing these added notes. It will produce a fuller and richer harmonic ending.

Ex. 41

IN STILLY NIGHT
(S. A. B.)

J. BRAHMS
Arr. by H. R. W.

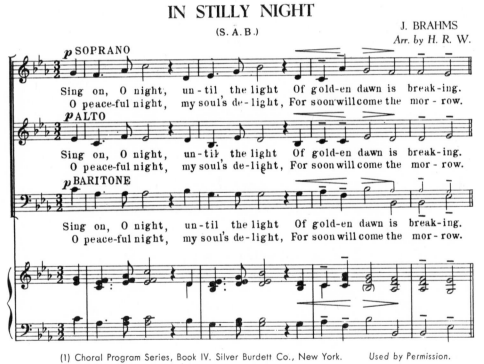

(1) Choral Program Series, Book IV. Silver Burdett Co., New York.   Used by Permission.

In writing for the SAB combination, it is often wise to give the bass part a considerable portion of the melody. First of all, it is easier for the boys to learn; secondly, the incomplete harmonies are not so obvious. Due to the limitations of ranges in young voices, it would seem natural for the voice parts to be more compact; however, since there is no tenor, as in the SATB combination, care must be taken to avoid wide spacing so that the harmony will sound solid.

The old masters were adept at writing for mixed combinations of three parts such as: SAB, STB, or SAT. They leaned heavily on counterpoint and melodic harmony, which should be a key to the arranger today, even though he is writing for young inexperienced voices. The arranger can well afford to study some of the compositions written for mixed voices in three parts to gain a better understanding of the possibilities of this combination.

Many choral directors and arrangers disparage the musical quality of this combination and, to be sure, it is not as effective as a fuller one. However, music can successfully be written for SAB and there certainly is a need.

SA(A-T)B COMBINATION

Many teachers and directors who dislike the three-part combination of SAB are continually seeking four-part material for the combination soprano, alto, alto-tenor, bass. The problems are the same as in four-part mixed voice writing, except for the limited range of the alto-tenor part. The young fellows with changing voices are given the unusual classification of alto-tenors. Their tone is generally fuzzy in quality and their range extends over about a sixth as follows: When writing for this combination the range for the basses is the same as in SAB.

SB COMBINATION

There has been very little written for just a combination of two parts using treble and changed voices, indicated as soprano-baritone, high-low, or girls and boys. However, there certainly is a field here which needs to be exploited because such a combination would ideally fit the needs of many schools. The staff-layout for such a combination is as follows:

Ex. 42 a

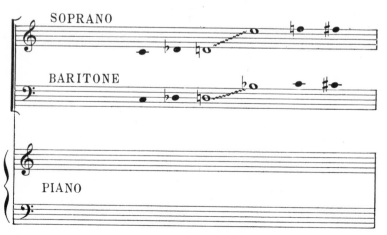

The writing that has been done for this combination is in two general styles. The first treats the voices as in two-part writing of the soprano-alto type; however, the soprano range is not so high as when writing for treble voices alone, the baritone singing the harmony notes usually given the alto part. The melody should often be given to the boys for variety and also for the different tonal effect of having the harmony above the melody. The following examples illustrate this style:

Ex. 42 **b**

ODE TO JOY

L. VAN BEETHOVEN
Arr. by H. R. W.

From Soprano-Baritone Choruses, Auditorium Series No. 37 Copyright 1939 Hall & McCreary Co., Chicago, Ill. Used by permission.

Ex. 43

IN THE SILVERY MOONLIGHT
(AU CLAIR DE LA LUNE)

Translation by H. R. W.

FRENCH FOLK SONG
Arr. by H. R. W.

From Soprano-Baritone Choruses, Auditorium Series No. 37
Copyright 1939 Hall & McCreary Co., Chicago, Ill.
Used by Permission

The second style of writing for this combination is to write a rhythmic passage for one part, usually the baritones; and have the sopranos sing the melody. The melody can be switched around in this style, also. The following arrangement is a very effective illustration of this style.

Ex. 44

COMIN' THRU THE RYE

Arr. by Harry Simione

This combination invariably needs an accompaniment unless the group is singing a canon or a section of an arrangement in canonic style. This need is evident because the baritones are not usually singing the fundamental bass and also because the harmonies are incomplete throughout the arrangement.

SATB COMBINATION DIVIDED

In writing for more than four mixed voices, there are two general styles, often referred to as polyvocal (many voices) and polychoric (many choirs). In the first of these styles, each voice part is divided into two or more sections; in the second, the entire group is divided into two or more choirs. Of course, sometimes there is an overlapping and general fusion of these two styles in one composition. The staves for the divided parts are indicated as in the first example in this chapter (Ex. 38).

As mentioned in the explanation of that example, only four staves are necessary, unless the part-writing is so contrapuntal or complicated that the vocal line and words are not clear unless a separate staff is used for each part. In the latter case, eight staves are required. When the music is written for two distinct choirs, two of the regular SATB staves are used and are indicated as Choir I and Choir II.

There are many combinations of voices which may be used in writing the polyvocal style. Here are a few of them:

SSATB—a favorite of Brahms.

SATBB—contra basses give an orchestral quality.

SSATBB—meets the problem of the fewer number of altos and tenors.

SSATTBB—a favorite of popular song groups; a girls' trio with male
      quartet.

Ex. 45

AT PARTING
S.S.A.T.B.B.

FREDERIC PETERSON   HARRY R. WILSON

The use of two distinct choirs is probably most effective in antiphonal singing in which Choir II, generally smaller and sometimes placed off stage, repeats the phrases sung by Choir I. The most famous example of this style of writing is Palestrina's "Gloria Patri." Bach makes use of two choirs in the final chorus, "Here Yet Awhile" from the St. Matthew's Passion. However, he has both choirs sing the same four-part contrapuntal harmony except in phrases where the music seems to demand a division of the choirs. It is a beautiful example and should be studied by every choral arranger.

The writing of eight parts in homophonic style, where the male voices and treble voices answer each other (in the same manner as the choirs of an orchestra) makes an effective setting. This procedure should not be continued too long because it can become tedious very quickly. Even though this style is polyvocal, most amateur choruses have little trouble with it. Here is a good example: (See also Ex. 11).

Ex. 46

LET THY HOLY PRESENCE
S.S.A.T.T.B.B.
(A Cappella)

P. TSCHESNOKOFF
Edited and Arr.
NOBLE CAIN

Except for the sophisticated arrangements of popular songs, the choral arranger has little use of more than four parts with an occasional *divisi.* Folk songs do not usually need more than four parts for their adequate expression unless they are sung unaccompanied with rhythmic effects. The arranging of art songs seldom calls for more than four parts because they generally have an instrumental accompaniment.

It is the choral composer who sometimes needs a larger combination of voices to express his musical ideas. Of the earlier composers, it is worth studying the works of Giovanni Gabrielli to see how he wrote for large vocal combinations. His "Jubilate Deo" still has a modern ring. The unlimited possibilities in voice combinations can be studied in Vaughan William's "Serenade to Music" written for sixteen solo voices and Healy Willan's "An Apostrophe to the Heavenly Hosts" where he uses two four-part mixed choirs and two 'mystic choirs', one four-part mixed and the other three-part treble.

When a choral arranger decides to use more than four voice parts, except for an occasional *divisi,* he must realize that he is automatically limiting the number of amateur choirs that will have the personnel to sing his arrangements. Therefore, he should ask himself if the added voice parts are necessary for adequate musical expression.

CHAPTER VI

CHORUS OF TREBLE VOICES

The word "treble" is used in this chapter in preference to 'girls',' 'women's,' or 'female's' because the discussion is to include any treble voice group, including boys' choirs of unchanged voices. Moreover, many school treble choirs include both boys and girls. It is true that, of all the types of singing groups, there are far more girls' glee clubs than any other combination. Every high school and college has a girls' chorus, and now many women's clubs, musical and otherwise, are forming singing groups. In fact, writing for treble voice groups is the largest single outlet for a choral arranger's wares. It is probably the fastest way of gaining the attention of the publishers.

Of course, there are definite artistic limitations in writing for these groups. The total range is small and the monochrome (one color) quality of all the parts produces a monotonous musical effect. Therefore, writing for these groups should be limited to rather short numbers, extended arrangements being questionable unless enriched with an interesting orchestral accompaniment or male voice solo. Nevertheless, all choral arrangers and composers should know the problems of writing for these groups because to secure tonal variety in mixed-voice writing, sections of a composition are often arranged for treble voices alone.

Regardless of the number of parts, whether two, three, or four, it is usually best to have a staff for each part. Naturally, G clefs are employed on all staves.

Ex. 47

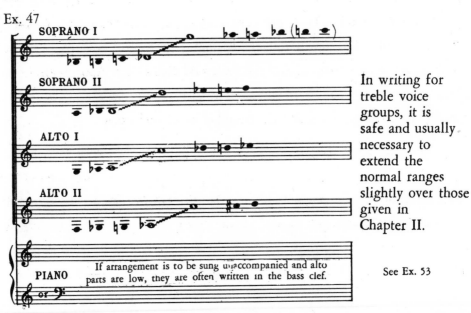

In writing for treble voice groups, it is safe and usually necessary to extend the normal ranges slightly over those given in Chapter II.

If arrangement is to be sung unaccompanied and alto parts are low, they are often written in the bass clef.

See Ex. 53

SSA COMBINATION

Arrangements of treble voices are generally written for Soprano I, Soprano II, and Alto (three staves, one staff for each voice) plus accompaniment. The parts are sometimes indicated as 'High,' 'Medium,' and 'Low' so as to avoid any resentment on the part of the "big fellows" of being labelled sopranos and altos. This combination probably evolved because of the shortages of second altos in the schools. In writing for SSA, it is never wise to take the altos lower than G below middle C, it being best to limit the low range to A♭ except in soft work. Naturally, this limitation necessitates extension of the upper range of all parts one or two semi-tones. However, most treble voice groups are sufficiently well-trained to assimilate this slight increase of tessitura.

All the ingenuity that an arranger has is needed in order to write interesting music for these groups. Special effort should be exercised to make all parts melodic; also, rhythmical variety shall be employed between them. The contrapuntal style is especially needed when the piece is to be sung unaccompanied. Mendelssohn's "Lift Thine Eyes" from 'Elijah' is one of the most excellent examples of music written for this combination without accompaniment. The entire piece is included here in condensed score form for thorough study.

Ex. 48 **a**

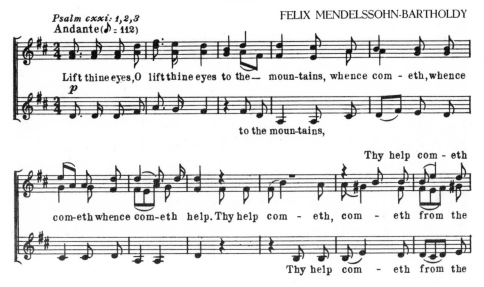

LIFT THINE EYES
(S.S.A.)

Psalm cxxi: 1,2,3
Andante (♪ = 112)

FELIX MENDELSSOHN-BARTHOLDY

Ex. 48 a

First inversions of triads sound exceptionally well for this combination. Many composers have used them in a parallel sweep, such as the following excerpt of Gaul's "At Eventide It Shall Be Light" from 'The Holy City.' This type of progression has become rather common, however. For the most part, this composition is written in the same style as the foregoing Mendelssohn number and is equally worthy of thorough study.

Ex. 48 b

AT EVENTIDE, IT SHALL BE LIGHT
(From "The Holy City")

A. R. GAUL

From Choral Program Series, Book II
Silver Burdett Co., New York
Used by Permission

When writing for this combination in 'a cappella' style, a 'divisi' of the altos at the final cadence gives a more complete chord if the lower part takes the fundamental note.

Ex. 49

OFT IN THE STILLY NIGHT
(S.S.A. a cappella)

IRISH AIR
Arr. by H. R. W.

Copyright Carl Fischer, Inc., New York   Used by permission.

Most usually, arrangements for this combination should have piano accompaniments (see Chapter VIII for the various styles). The piano accompaniment provides the fundamental bass, especially for the ending, as well as a richer musical texture for the entire piece. However, where the contrapuntal style is employed (as, for example, in the three preceding excerpts) and the treatment of the parts is sufficiently interesting, no accompaniment is necessary.

When an accompaniment is used, the addition of other instruments, such as one or two violins, flutes, trumpets, etc., creates greater musical variety, as in the following example:

SOMEWHERE A CHILD IS SINGING

Ex. 50

S.S.A.

With optional obbligato for violin (or flute)
and, if feasible, a second violin

Text and Music by
PETER W. DYKEMA

All the devices suggested in previous chapters may be used in arranging for SSA, namely, shifting of the melody, use of canon, contrapuntal lines, rhythmic effects, humming, neutral vowels, discontinuance and overlapping of parts, descants, solos; all contributing to a more interesting arrangement.

SA COMBINATION

Although most choral directors of girls' glee clubs seem to prefer the SSA combination, there have been many fine duets written for soprano and alto which sound extremely well when sung by treble choral groups. An example of most successful writing for the SA combination is found in Pergolesi's, "Stabat Mater," written for soprano-alto with orchestral accompaniment. Here is one short excerpt.

Ex. 51

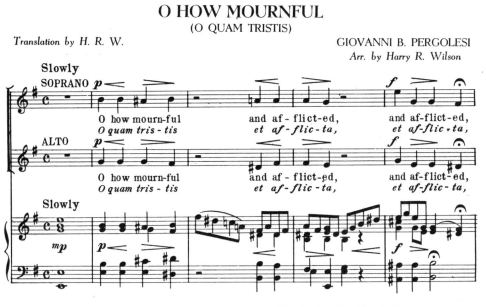

O HOW MOURNFUL
(O QUAM TRISTIS)

Translation by H. R. W.

GIOVANNI B. PERGOLESI
Arr. by Harry R. Wilson

From Choral Program Series, Book I, Silver Burdett Co., New York
Used by Permission

Another excellent example of writing (in the modern idiom) for this combination is "A Ceremony of Carols" by the English composer Benjamin Britten (pub. by Boosey & Hawkes, Inc.).

Since only two notes of the chord are represented, arrangements for the SA combination should have an accompaniment unless the piece is in canonic style. The accompaniment should be colorful but in keeping with the lightness of the vocal tone. The writing of an optional descant for selected voices introduced near the close gives an added part and a fuller ending without placing unreasonable demands upon the vocal facilities of the choral group (as in the following).

Ex. 52

LISTEN TO THE LAMBS

NEGRO SPIRITUAL
Arr. by H. R. W.

From Choral Program Series, Book I, Silver Burdett Co., New York
Used by Permission

For this combination, it is not wise to write for the alto below
A [musical notation] or the soprano above F# or G. [musical notation] Often, parts are
simply indicated as 'High' and 'Low' to avoid any resentment of the boys
for having to sing parts marked 'Soprano' or 'Alto,' which, to them, represents something to be done by girls.

In writing for the SA combination, the most euphonious intervals are
the third and the sixth. However, an occasional fourth or fifth, or the dis-
sonance of the second, is often a relief from the continual sweetness of the
third and sixth. Contrapuntal and canonic writing are especially gracious in
a combination of two voices and part of every arrangement should include
one of these styles.

It is questionable taste, except in the folk songs of the Latin-American
countries, to use the soprano as a tenor part when the alto is singing the
melody. Many of the Latin-American songs employ continual thirds sung
by two parts. Such continual use of the same interval obscures the melody
and consequently it loses its identity. This style is indigenous with some of
the songs of these countries; however, the same device used for the folk
songs of other countries will cause them to lose their native character.

There is a need for fine SA arrangements for choral performance aside
from the incidental arrangements found in school songbooks. Arrangers will
usually find a cordial reception from the publishers if they master the musical
limitations of this combination and are able to write effective numbers for it.

SSAA COMBINATION

The most satisfactory sounding combination for treble voices is SSAA. The four parts offer an opportunity for complete chords with the fundamental, although the second alto quality cannot in anyway be considered as a bass. The number of choral groups which will attempt arrangements for this combination are limited. This is due to the shortage of altos who can sing low notes with a deep, rich quality. To offset this limitation, it is necessary to extend the normal range of the first sopranos to G or A♭ in writing for this combination.

Since complete four-part harmony is possible, the SSAA combination lends itself to unaccompanied writing better than any of the other treble voice combinations. Nevertheless, it is not wise to write extended arrangements for SSAA without accompaniment because there still remains the monochrome tonal quality of treble voices alone.

Brahms wrote a number of choral pieces for the SSAA combination, constructed on a sound harmonic bass but each part an interesting and singable melodic line. They are all worth serious study. The following excerpt is a complete verse of one of the loveliest of these pieces. It is written with accompaniment but may be sung a cappella.

Ex. 53

LOVE SONG
S.S.A.A.

English Text Adapted
by H. R. W.

JOHANNES BRAHMS
Edited by Harry R. Wilson

From Choral Program Series Book II Silver Burdett Co., New York   Used by Permission

Ex.53 Cont.

CONCLUSION

Much missionary work is needed to influence treble glee clubs to sing in four parts (SSAA)) instead of the usual three parts (SSA). Many more musical arrangements that are worthwhile should be written for the four-part combination. Any glee club that has the technical proficiency to sing in three parts can sing in four parts if the slightly extended range of the outside parts can be surmounted. If arrangers realize and study the possibilities of this combination, and learn how to write well for it, perhaps they can provide directors with much needed material which their singing groups can master.

CHAPTER VII

CHORUS OF MALE VOICES

When we speak of a chorus of male voices we refer to changed voices. Unchanged boys' voices come under the problem of treble choirs. Although male glee clubs have a monochrome effect (as in treble choirs), the quality of the voices is so rich and vibrant that it is more feasible to write longer works for male voices than for treble.

In writing for a chorus of male voices, it is sometimes necessary to extend the normal range of the first tenors and second basses a semitone beyond the range indicated in Chapter II. The use of the *falsetto* in the tenor voice, for high *pianissimo* passages, not only gives an extended range of several semitones, but also, an additional quality of tone which can be used with unique effect. The Russian male choirs are especially adept in the use of the *falsetto* for unusual musical effects. The usual staves and clefs for male voice writing are as follows:

Ex. 54

TTBB COMBINATION (STANDARD)

Of all the combinations of voices, treble or mixed, the four-part male glee club lends itself best to unaccompanied singing. This is due partly to the quality of voices, but mostly, to the compactness of harmony in a low range.

In the standard style of writing for the TTBB combination the melody is normally in the first tenor. When the melody is shifted to one of the lower parts, the upper parts are usually written in a contrapuntal style. It is impossible to avoid continual crossing of parts without shifting the melody because of the closeness of the harmony. To avoid this continual crossing of parts, some arrangers often shift the melody for just a few notes, even for only one or two. When this is done the melody becomes lost. As was suggested in writing for other combinations of voices, it is best not to shift the melody for less than a musical phrase. The crossing of parts is usually found in the first tenor moving below the second tenor to carry the lower notes of the melody, the two parts seeming to interchange for a time. This crossing, when used, should be done gracefully, as regards the melodic lines of the two parts. It occurs most often at the closing cadences when the melody descends. The following example illustrates the crossing of the tenor parts at the cadence:

Ex. 55

AT PARTING
FOR MEN'S VOICES
(A Cappella)

FREDERIC PETERSON   HARRY R. WILSON

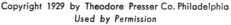

Humming is especially effective as an accompaniment to the melody or a soloist. Descants, as such, are practically never written. Canonic writing automatically produces continual crossing of parts which, however, is easy, sounds natural, and is very effective. In writing for male voices there is always the tendency to write the lush harmony produced by over-chromaticism. This gives the effect of "barber-shop" writing and should be avoided unless this effect is deliberately intended. Rhythmical and sound effects seem especially appropriate in writing for male voices and, as a novelty, even whistling might be introduced, although purists would probably say that the arranger was departing from anything that resembled music.

TTBB COMBINATION (BARBER-SHOP)

The famous American style of singing labelled "barber-shop" or "curbstone" harmony is probably the only style of singing which has an association designed to preserve its existence, namely, the SPEBSQSA (The Society for the Preservation and Extension of Barber-Shop Quartet Singing in America). Although this style of singing is often frowned upon by serious composers as being banal and over-saccarine, the fact remains that it is greatly enjoyed by most amateur groups. It is true that the style best fits the old-time popular music and has no place in the more serious style of writing.

In barber-shop writing the melody is invariably in the second tenor, so the parts are often called top tenor, lead, baritone, and bass. In many barbershop quartets the harmonies are faked, that is, sung without the aid of notes. In writing a number in this style to be sung by a male quartet or glee club, the arranger should try to retain the same spontaneous harmonic quality. A little participation on his own part in some barber-shop singing will give him an instinctive feel for the parts.

Humming may be used but very seldom. Canonic and contrapuntal writing have little place. Descants are a foreign language. Close harmony prevails. Chromaticism comes into its own. The *portamento* style of the singing opens up vistas of the possibilities of divided semitones. Keys must be carefully chosen with regard to keeping the melody preponderantly in the lead tenor so as to retain the individuality of this style. All types of rhythmic effects are good. There is a continual crossing of the second tenor and baritone parts but this does not cause confusion. The other parts practically never cross. Occasionally, it is necessary to shift the melody to the first tenor but in so doing the purity of the style is somewhat lost. Here is a typical example of barber-shop harmony:

Ex. 56

TELL ME WHY

ANONYMOUS
Arr. by Harry R. Wilson

From Choral Program Series, Book IV, Silver Burdett Co., New York
Used by Permission

The following excerpts, taken from a modern arrangement in modified barber-shop style, indicate possible devices and procedures:

Ex. 57

THE WHIFFENPOOF SONG
(BAA! BAA! BAA!)
GLEE CLUB T.T.B.B.

Revision by
RUDY VALLEE

By
MEADE MINNERGERODE
GEORGE POMEROY
TOD B. GALLOWAY
Arr. by H. R. W.

(THE WHIFFENPOOF SONG - later section)

Ex. 58

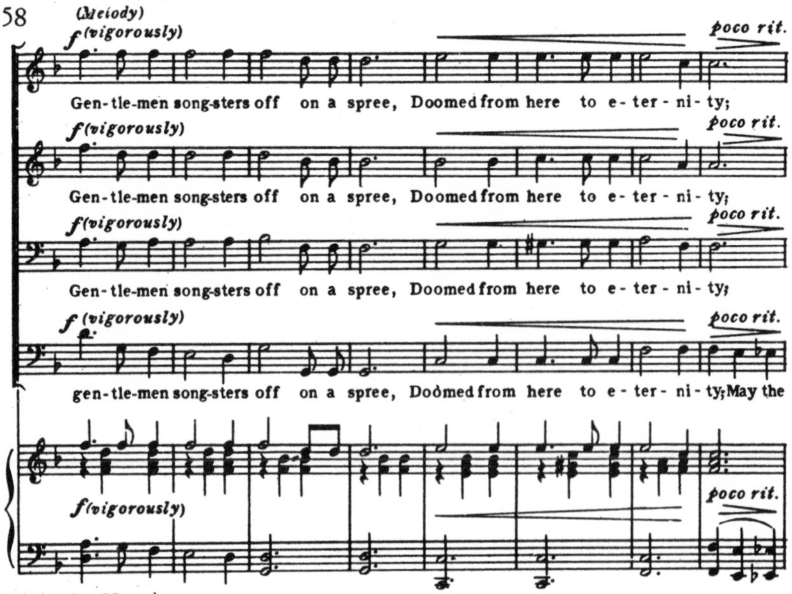

(Melody)
f (vigorously)
poco rit.
Gen-tle-men song-sters off on a spree, Doomed from here to e-ter-ni-ty;
f (vigorously)
poco rit.
Gen-tle-men song-sters off on a spree, Doomed from here to e-ter-ni-ty;
f (vigorously)
poco rit.
Gen-tle-men song-sters off on a spree, Doomed from here to e-ter-ni-ty;
f (vigorously)
poco rit.
gen-tle-men song-sters off on a spree, Doomed from here to e-ter-ni-ty; May the
f (vigorously)
poco rit.

Ex. 59 (In Verse)

Medium Voice Solo
Yes, the mag-ic of their sing-ing of the songs we love so
TENOR I
pp
Hm,
TENOR II
pp
Hm,
BASS I
pp
Hm,
BASS II
pp
Hm,
well "Shall I Wast-ing," and "Ma-vour-neen", and the rest;
mp
and the rest;
mp
and the rest;
mp
and the rest;
mp
and the rest;

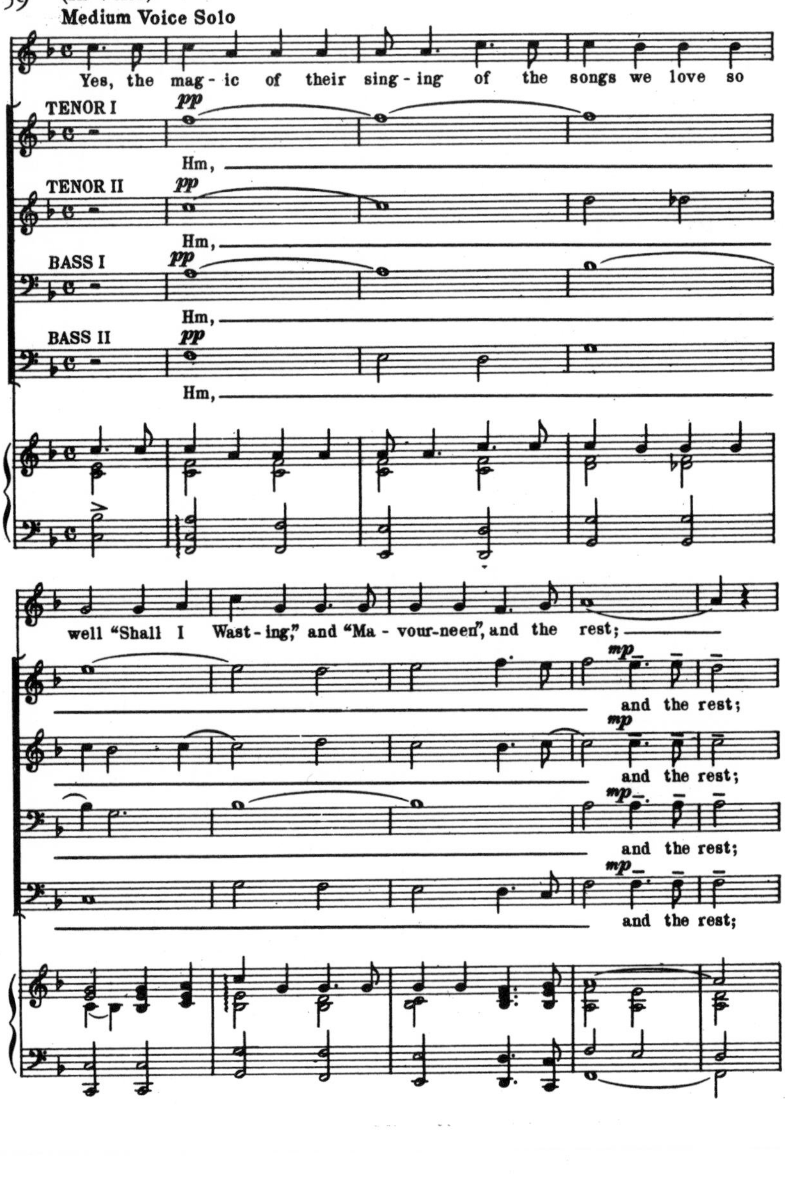

Ex. 60 (THE WHIFFENPOOF SONG - 2nd chorus)

Another style of barber-shop writing is for the lead (or second) tenor to sing a phrase as a solo while the other parts join in on the second phrase of the period. This procedure is especially appropriate for humorous or dialect songs. As a rule, all parts join together on the refrain. Here is an excerpt to illustrate this style.

Ex. 61

R. H. H.

WHO DAT A-CALLIN' ME?

RUTH HUFFMAN HUNT
Edited by Harry R. Wilson

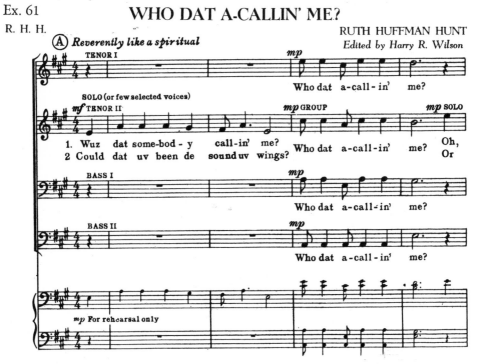

From Choral Program Series Book III Silver Burdett Co., Chicago By Permission

It is at the closing cadences that barber-shop harmony comes into its own. All kinds of weird changes may be experimented with. Practically anything goes as long as the final triad is reached by all voices at the same time. Many arrangers, including the writer, are much more conservative in the writing of barber-shop cadences because the style can easily be carried to the point of bad taste. Here are some of the endings often sung by barber-shop quartets. Ex. 62

SWEET ADELINE CADENCE

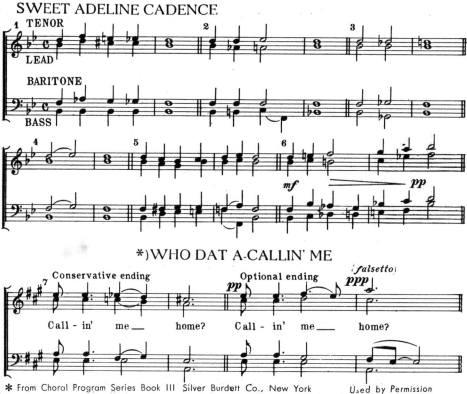

*)WHO DAT A-CALLIN' ME

* From Choral Program Series Book III Silver Burdett Co., New York   Used by Permission

TBB COMBINATION

Due to the shortage of first tenors a considerable amount of experimenting is being done in writing for three-part male choruses. Sometimes the three parts are indicated as TTB (tenor, tenor, bass) but it is more consistent to label the combination TBB (tenor, baritone, bass). Although this combination lacks the fullness and richness of TTBB arrangements, some fine compositions have been written for TBB, as exemplified by the following classic excerpt:

Ex. 63

VERE LANGUORES NOSTRES *
T.B.B.

ANTONIO LOTTI

*Originally in
G minor for T.T.B.

From Choral Program Series Book III
Silver Burdett Co., New York
Used by Permission

Usually the arrangements for this combination are designed for glee clubs of boys and young men, therefore, it is wise to reduce the voice ranges for the various parts. The staves and most practical vocal ranges are as follows.

Ex. 64

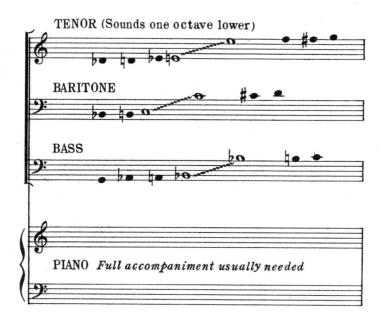

All of the various suggestions made in Chapter III to make arrangements interesting are effective in writing for this combination. There need not be as much crossing of parts in the TBB arrangement as in the TTBB, due to the elimination of one inner part which causes the harmony to be somewhat more 'spread.' Since these arrangements are for young voices, it is wise to avoid crossing of parts unless the style is contrapuntal or canonic.

The barber-shop style of writing calls for four-parts; therefore, arrangements for the TBB combination will follow closely the style of writing for the standard TTBB combination. However, a semblance of the barber-shop style can be attained wherever it is desired and appropriate. A considerable amount of unison is good because it is learned more easily by young groups. It is also effective to have different phrases of the melody sung in unison by various combinations of parts.

If the melody is in the tenor and descends, say as low as F, the final cadence may cause trouble since then the baritone and bass parts are too low and a unison ending becomes necessary. When the ending is an ascending cadence, a chord with two roots (tenor and bass) and a third (baritone) is the usual result. A complete chordal ending can be attained by dividing the tenors on the last chord, giving the fifth to the second tenor. When the baritone is carrying the melody, the basses may divide on the last chord to give a complete chordal ending. Since the bass in the TBB combination is treated as a *fundamental* bass, the endings are not written as in the SSA combination. These various endings are illustrated by the following examples. Condensed scores are used to save space.

Ex. 65

THE ANGLER'S SONG
T.B.B.
Arr. by H. R. W.

BATTLE OF JERICHO
Arr. by H. R. W.

MASTERS IN THE HALL   VERE LANGUORES NOSTRES
LOTTI

From Choral Program Series Book III   Silver Burdett Co., New York   Used by Permission

There is no question that, if a glee club can handle TTBB arrangements, it should not sing TBB numbers except where compositions are especially written for this combination, such as example No. 63. Since many schools cannot handle the four-part male arrangements (because of a serious lack of first tenors and second basses), their male glee clubs are dependent upon TBB arrangements; or, very simple compositions for TTBB with limited voice ranges.

TB COMBINATION

Arrangements for this combination (tenor-baritone) are designed for boys glee clubs that lack the vocal equipment with which to sing TTBB or TBB arrangements. At times, a composition may lend itself to two-part writing for changed male voices, as in songs for tenor and baritone duets. The latter, however, are usually too pretentious for young male glee clubs to perform.

The voice ranges for this combination must be kept as narrow as posible within the scope of the musical expression desired. The following ranges are usable.

Ex. 66

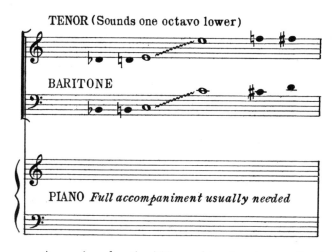

Arranging for the TB combination is usually done in one of two styles. It is often treated as an SA combination singing one octave lower. In this style there is no attempt to make the baritone a fundamental bass but rather to treat it as an alto part. The other style is to treat the TB combination as a male voice combination (TTBB) with the lower parts omitted. Here the baritone part usually carries the melody; the tenor part sings in the usual tenor idiom. Both of these styles can be used in the same arrangement for contrast.

The following examples show the general treatment of the parts in both styles. Of course, the Brahms' number was written especially for this combination. Although part of its beauty is dependent upon the lovely accompaniment, the parts themselves are worthy of concentrated study.

Ex. 67

LOVE SONG
(LIEBESLIEDER No. 14)

English Text by H. R. W.

JOHANNES BRAHMS
Edited by *Harry R. Wilson*

From Choral Program Series Book III
Silver Burdett Co., New York
Used by Permission

Ex. 68

HOME ON THE RANGE

Arr. by H. R. W.

From "SONGS OF HILLS & PLAINS"
Copyright 1943 Hall & McCreary Co., Chicago   Used by Permission

Two-part contrapuntal and canonic devices, which the author has been pointing out throughout the book, should permeate the writing in the two styles illustrated above. These devices are best shown by an example such as the following:

MASTERS IN THE HALL

OLD FRENCH CAROL
Arr. by H.R.W.

From Choral Program Series Book III   Silver Burdett Co. New York   Used by Permission

It is wise to use considerable unison in arranging for the TB combination, to be sung by both parts or shifted between parts. Closing cadence problems occur in the same way as in TBB combination and the same solutions are appropriate. One caution should be observed, that is: writing for TB should never be thought of as just a melody and a fundamental bass with the inner parts missing. Of course, this effect may be used if desired but, as a rule, it is empty and bizarre. The TB combination invariably needs a piano accompaniment except, possibly, for contrapuntal or canonic sections.

CONCLUSION

Good, easy, and singable arrangements are needed for young male glee clubs. It is difficult to interest boys in singing, but one sure way is to organize a male glee club, and the constant cry is for material written especially for them.

There may be occasions where an arranger wishes to divide the male voices into more than four parts to retain the harmony of the original piece. This is exceptional, however, because of the lowness and closeness of the harmony, more than four parts become too "muddy" in color. Besides most glee clubs have enough trouble with TTBB arrangements and compositions. (See "Temptation," ex. No. 4.)

CHAPTER VIII

THE ACCOMPANIMENT

It is the opinion of the author, after examining hundreds of choral manuscripts submitted to him by students, that it is in the writing of piano accompaniments where most novice arrangers meet their nemesis. The effectiveness of interesting vocal lines can be completely spoiled by an amateurish accompaniment. Every choral arranger should study the vocal and choral works of such masters as Robert Schumann and observe his skill in writing varied types of accompaniments that are musically interesting.

Of course, the easiest way to avoid the writing of 'bad' accompaniments is to arrange all numbers to be sung *a cappella* (or unaccompanied). However, as mentioned in the previous chapters, certain combinations of voices, such as SA, SSA, TB, TTB, SB, and SAB, usually need an accompaniment to fill in the missing harmonies and provide added musical interest. Writing unaccompanied arrangements for any combination of voices requires a skilled hand to make the voice parts sufficiently interesting to stand alone.

ACCOMPANIMENT FOR REHEARSAL ONLY

Usually, when a choral number is arranged for *a cappella* singing, an accompaniment which is a duplication of the voice parts is included on the manuscript. This is only intended as an aid, "For Rehearsal Only" and is often engraved in small notes. The same practice is followed where, in compositions that have an accompaniment, certain sections are to be sung *a cappella*. The following example illustrates this procedure:

Ex. 70

HE NEVER SAID A MUMBALIN' WORD
(EIGHT PART MIXED CHORUS)

Spiritual Arr. by
HARRY R. WILSON

As a rule, few choral arrangers today feel the necessity of an accompaniment which just duplicates the voice parts, except to facilitate learning the piece at rehearsals. Most directors, also, prefer to have arrangements sung unaccompanied when they are so intended; however, because of the flatting in pitch of their singers, they often resort, out of desperation, to the use of a piano accompaniment.

OPTIONAL ACCOMPANIMENT

Some arrangements, notably those for SSA, TBB, and SAB, even for SATB, call for a degree of support of the voice parts, even though they are musically satisfying in themselves. In such cases an optional accompaniment is often written. These accompaniments may or may not be used at the discretion of the director. They usually follow the rhythmical and chordal pattern of the voice parts, but fill in the missing harmonies and further enrich the harmony by using fuller chords in the right hand and often octaves in the bass. The following excerpt illustrates an optional accompaniment for a simple SAB composition:

Ex. 71

GOD BE IN MY HEAD

Words from the
SARUM PRIMER, (1588)

H. R. W.

RHYTHMICAL ACCOMPANIMENTS

Many folk-songs of a lively nature need only a simple rhythmical accompaniment to bring out their spirit. This type of rhythm is sometimes called an "oom-pah" accompaniment. It is often embellished when used as an accompaniment in published arrangements. This favorite play-party song is an example:

SKIP TO MY LOU

American Dance Tune
Arr. by H. R. W.

Of course, there are other types of rhythmical accompaniment which are appropriate, especially in the arranging of folk dances or popular songs. The arranger must be careful that a rhythmical accompaniment does not become monotonous. He can avoid this by employing figuration while retaining the basic rhythmical pattern. Here are several styles of rhythmical accompaniment:

Ex. 73

HOLIDAY PARADE
Four Part S.A.T.B.

Words by
MITCHELL PARISH

Music by
DOMENICO SAVINO

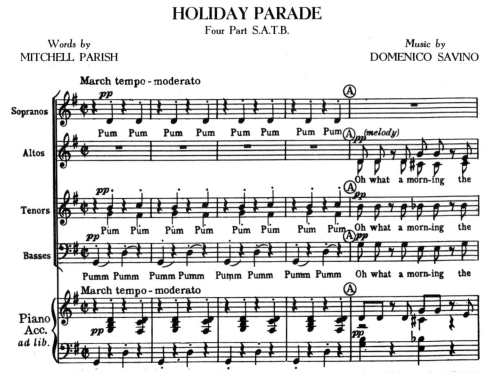

Ex. 74

A HEART THAT'S FREE
(S. S. A.)

A. G. ROBYN
Arr. by Hugo Frey

BLUE MOON
Three Part S. S. A.

Lyric by
LORENZ HART

Music by
RICHARD RODGERS
Arr. by Hugo Frey

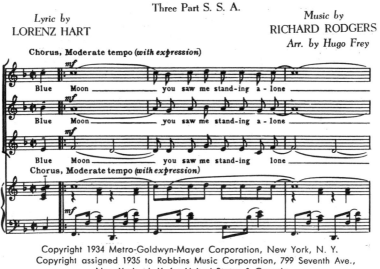

MELODIC ACCOMPANIMENTS

A favorite style of accompaniment to support the voice parts, and, at the same time add a little musical interest, is the practice of playing the melody in either the right or left hand of the piano part. This procedure makes the piano part almost a little composition in itself. It supports the voices and, although not distinct from them, has individual musical interest. This practice is invariably followed in the arranging of popular songs although it is by no means limited to them. The melody is often switched in the piano part in the same manner as in the voice parts. The following short excerpt is typical:

Ex. 76

THOSE HOURS WITH YOU
(S.S.A.)

Words and Music by
HARRY ROBERT WILSON

EMBELLISHING ACCOMPANIMENTS

The master composers of song have given us the best examples of florid accompaniments. They are of all types but are usually based upon some kind of *arpeggio* figuration. In writing these types of accompaniments, the arranger should be careful that they are an integral part of the composition and not just a display of piano technique with little relation to the musical expression of the voice parts.

In using *arpeggios* as the basis for accompaniments, the arranger should be sure to hold them in place with a fundamental bass, otherwise, they will seem to be at loose ends and almost fly off of the manuscript paper. In other words, don't depend too much upon the pianist's artistic use of the sustaining pedal to make the accompaniment sound. All the necessary notes and their duration should be plainly indicated.

Ex. 77

DEDICATION
(TO SINFONIANS EVERYWHERE)
OP. 25 No. 1

English Text
by Harry R. Wilson

ROBERT SCHUMANN
Arr. by J. Hubert Liverman

From Choral Program Series Book III
Silver Burdett Co., New York
Used by Permission

DIFFICULT ACCOMPANIMENTS

The foregoing section suggests a caution about the writing of difficult accompaniments. The skill of the accompanist of most amateur choirs is often limited. The arranger who writes piano accompaniments that require virtuosity is borrowing trouble. It is a keen disappointment for a choral director to train his group to render an expressive and musical performance of the voice parts and then have the effectiveness marred by the inability of the accompanist to play the accompaniment. The same is true of band and orchestral accompaniments. Naturally, the accompaniment must be musically adequate but should be playable by the average pianist.

INDEPENDENT ACCOMPANIMENTS

Some arrangers and composers have written accompaniments which are partially, or even totally, independent of the voices and still effect a satisfying musical expression. This type of accompaniment is usually found in original compositions rather than arrangements. As long as the two (accompaniment and voice) form a synchronized whole, the result is musically pleasing. When the accompaniment completely absorbs the musical interest, the singers often have a feeling of futility which distracts from their performance. This type of accompaniment should only be attempted after much experience in composing or arranging.

For instance, the accompaniment of the Liebeslieder Waltzes of Brahms sound extremely well as a piano duet, but still, when the choral parts are sung with this completely independent four-hand piano accompaniment, the dual result is a unified artistic composition of musical charm. The following is an excerpt from one of these waltzes:

Ex. 78

LOVE WALTZ
(LIEBESLIEDER No. 13)

Translated by H. R. W.

JOHANNES BRAHMS

From Choral Program Series Book I
Silver Burdett Co., New York
Used by Permission

FOUR-HAND ACCOMPANIMENTS (ONE PIANO)

The foregoing example illustrates the possibilities of using four-hand accompaniments, a type of accompaniment that has been greatly neglected in choral writing. It is true that another piano staff per page needs to be engraved and publishers are continually thinking of costs and practicability. However, the musical effectiveness of an expanded accompaniment would certainly offset these objections where an arrangement would be enhanced by a four-hand accompaniment. Moreover, every chorus usually has among its ranks some member who can assist the regular accompanist by playing the *secondo* part.

It so happens that one of the most successful choral arrangements of recent times utilizes a four-hand accompaniment of considerable ingenuity. The following excerpts are from this arrangement:

Ex. 79

BATTLE HYMN OF THE REPUBLIC

Music by
WILLIAM STEFFE

Poem by
JULIA HOWE
Arr. by Roy Ringwald

Ex. 80

TWO-PIANO ACCOMPANIMENTS

There is a similar need in choral writing for arrangements with a two-piano accompaniment. By the use of two pianos, an orchestral solidity can be secured. The problem here *is* practical. It is difficult for many schools to have two pianos that are in tune, or have some semblance of tonal balance available on one stage. Many schools are lucky to have one piano — two are usually out of the question. Thus, a two-piano accompaniment greatly limits the possibilities of performance. Most choral compositions which require a two-piano accompaniment are usually published also in an edition in which the accompaniment is reduced so that it can be played on one piano (by one pianist). Unless this can be done, it seems wise for an arranger to confine his expanded accompaniments to four hands using one piano.

PIANO ACCOMPANIMENT WITH INSTRUMENTS

Most schools have an instrumental organization, either band or orchestra. If not, there are usually a few instrumental players around the school who are eager for a chance to perform. It would be advantageous for choral directors to make use of these players. However, there are very few choral arrangements which call for a small number of instruments with the piano as an accompaniment.

In Chapter VI the advantages of using one or two instruments with treble voices was pointed out. There are unlimited possibilities in this area and, if such arrangements were made available, they would probably be popular with choral directors.

A list of instrumental combinations which could be used with piano to add to the musical interest of choral arrangements would include: two violins; two trumpets; violin and cello; violin, viola and cello; brass quartets of different combinations, especially with male voices; two flutes; flute and clarinet; two clarinets; two French horns; harp; and tympani. It is obvious that the possibilities are practically unlimited. Choral accompaniments which include additional instruments often afford a delightful relief from the uniform color of singing voices. A few examples will show how some composers have made use of such accompaniments:

Ex. 81

SONG FROM OSSIAN'S FINGAL

J. BRAHMS

100

Weep, oh thou maid - en of I - ni - store!

Weep, oh thou maid - en of I - ni - store!

Weep, oh thou maid - en of I - ni - store!

Ex. 82

BEFORE THE PALING OF THE STARS
S.S.A.A.
(SOPRANO SOLO AND TWO TRUMPETS)
ad libitum

CHRISTINA ROSETTI

ERNEST KANITZ

SOLO

hail the King of Glo - ry, To hail the

SOPRANO I

hail the King of Glo - ry, To hail the

SOPRANO II

hail the King of Glo - ry, To hail the King, the

ALTO I

hail the King of Glo - ry, To hail the King of Glo - ry,

ALTO II

hail the King of Glo - ry, of Glo - ry, the

Tpts.(Bb)

BAND AND ORCHESTRAL ACCOMPANIMENTS

Music educators are continuously urging directors of choral and instrumental groups to combine their efforts for the added educational and musical values to the participants. This idea is gradually gaining converts and more and more regular programs as well as festival programs contain, at least, one choral number with band or orchestral accompaniment. The author makes a practice of including one number of this nature on the numerous programs which he conducts.

As in the case with the piano accompaniment, the director does not usually have a professional orchestra or band at his disposal. The technique of the players is often limited, and also, there is usually insufficient rehearsal time for the instrumental accompaniment. Moreover, the combined rehearsals of singers and instruments are usually hurried affairs. Therefore, during the *writing* of the instrumental accompaniment, the arranger or composer should use all his ingenuity to insure adequate results with such limited means.

The arranger would be wise to consider carefully a few other cautions. Avoid any accompaniment which may be too heavy for immature or undeveloped amateur voices. Avoid needless technical difficulties when a simpler solution will be just as effective. Avoid the extreme ranges of instruments, which invite "out of tune" playing, especially in the woodwinds. It is well to provide a generous supply of optional, as well as cued-in, parts in anticipation of the instruments which may be missing in the ensemble.

Practically every school has a creditable band although the orchestra may be meager and struggling. Still, orchestral accompaniments are far more available than those for band. Regardless of the musical superiority of the orchestra as an accompaniment for voices, there is a practical need for more choral numbers with band accompaniment. It is beyond the scope of this book to discuss the techniques of arranging for amateur bands and orchestras. The reader is referred to such books as Paul Yoder's, "Arranging for the School Band," Robbins Music Corp., and A. O. Andersen's, "Practical Orchestration," C. C. Birchard and Co.

CONCLUSION

At the risk of being redundant, the author wishes to close this chapter with a statement similar to the one which he made in the beginning. So often in arranging for amateur choral groups (and most of them are amateur) it is the accompaniment which may be the deciding factor in the success or failure of the arrangement. So often the choral arranger is likewise a choral director and has a natural feel for voice lines. Consequently, he needs to strengthen his techniques in writing musical accompaniments if his work is to possess professional flavor. In writing accompaniments the arranger should continually ask himself such questions as the following: Is the accompaniment pianistic? Does it lie well under the hands? Does it have rhythmical flow? Were the choral motives and figurations utilized in the accompaniment (see ex. 52)? A complete book could be written on this subject and so the author urges the reader to make a systematic study of the developments and styles in writing piano accompaniments for voices.

CHAPTER IX

THE TEXT

Since choral music is dependent upon words, the text must receive consideration equal to that given the music. The composer must choose his texts carefully because the literary quality of the words is usually reflected in the musical quality of the music. Fine poems beget fine music. Of course, some of the masters did write glorious music to some rather banal texts but this was because their genius rose above the mediocrity of the words.

SUITABILITY OF TEXTS

As mentioned in a previous chapter, the choral composer can turn to the bible, standard poetic works, or lyrics of recognized worth by modern poets. Some adaptation may become necessary when using literary works for musical settings. This is permissible provided the poetry is not mutilated. Some poetry, although fine as poetry, may not necessarily lend itself to a musical setting and is therefore best left alone. This decision we leave to the composer.

The writing of lyrics for a popular song is a professional job which very few amateurs can hope to do with success. There is nothing as bad as a bad popular lyric and the amateur composer who has ambitions to write in this field should seek professional collaboration.

Unlike the composer, the choral arranger, unless he is both composer and arranger of a song, has the words given to him along with the melody, and so it becomes a matter of the selection of suitable verses and an editorial job.

SINGABILITY OF TEXTS

Some excellent poems, although they are fine as literature, are not singable. All texts should literally sing themselves. Combinations of words containing double consonants are difficult to sing and do not foster lovely *legato* lines. The words must 'flow into each other' as in much of the poetry of Robert Burns. The following poem is an example of one which is so filled with double consonants that to set it to music would be a hazardous task.

Ex. 83

WORLD, TAKE GOOD NOTICE

World, take good notice, silver stars fading,
Milky hue ript, weft of white detaching,
Coals thirty-eight, baleful and burning,
Scarlet, significant, hands off warning,
Now and henceforth flaunt from these shores.
from "Leaves of Grass"—Walt Whitman

Nevertheless, many modern choral composers are turning to the free verse of Walt Whitman to best express their musical ideas. Many of the lines of his poetry have beautiful lyric quality. For example:

Ex. 84

a. 'Look down, fair moon, and bathe this scene.'
b. 'O, a new song, a free song.'
c. 'Out of the cradle endlessly rocking.'
d. 'I hear America singing.'

It is interesting to note that all of these poems have been used by well-known modern composers for musical settings.

As a rule, it is well to be careful of poems with too many sibilant consonants. Try singing, "Let us set sail on the bounteous sea." Try to avoid double consonants of 'd' followed by 'b' or 't' as in 'soothed by' or 'loud tone'; also, words ending in 't' when followed by a word beginning with 't' such as 'last time.' There are countless little rules and things to watch but the best practice is to read the words aloud to make sure they flow; and then, try singing them to a melody.

The following poem is the quintessence of an easy flow of words. So much so, in fact, that it seems like a song without a melody.

Ex. 85

Ode

WE ARE THE MUSIC MAKERS

(First Verse)

We are the music makers,
And we are the dreamers of dreams,
Wandering by lone sea-breakers,
And setting by desolate streams;—
World-losers and world-forsakers,
On whom the pale moon gleams:
Yet we are the movers and shakers
Of the world forever it seems.

A. O'Shaughnessy

When editing a text, the arranger should sing the various parts to see if the words flow easily in each part. Sometimes, the words sing well in one part but, due to the melodic construction of another part, they are clumsy. A slight rhythmical change in the part may correct the difficulty. At times, slight changes in the words, especially the unimportant ones, may produce a more even flow without impairing the poetry. Be as careful with the musical flow of the words as of the voice parts.

ACCENT OF WORDS AND MUSIC

In addition to the attention which must be given to the euphony of words, an equal amount of care must be devoted to having the accent of the words synchronize with the accent of the music within a bar. A composer should read and scan a poem many times until the natural inflection of the words suggests a meter and melodic line for the music.

The arranger must be just as careful, when arranging songs (especially folk-songs) for voice combinations. Securing agreement of musical accent with text presents a marked difficulty especially in contrapuntal writing, where the melodic lines of the lower or inner parts may need considerable rhythmic revision from their original form. If an arranger is careless in this, the inevitable result is an inartistic performance due to the unmusical phrasing and nuance. Also, since the response of singers is more spontaneous when there is a natural accent and rhythm of words, a failure to match accent of words and music often presents actual tonal and rhythmic difficulties.

The following examples may shed a little light on the problem.

Ex. 86

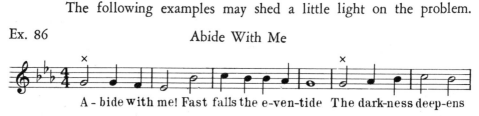

Abide With Me

A - bide with me! Fast falls the e-ven-tide The dark-ness deep-ens

In this old hymn, the accent of words and music do not coincide at places marked X. However, this fact did not deter its popularity.

Ex. 87

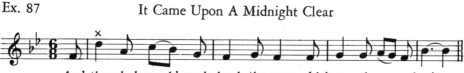

It Came Upon A Midnight Clear

And the whole world sends back the song which now the an-gels sing._

This unnatural accent comes in the last line of the third verse.

Ex. 88

Cradle Song

J. Brahms

Lull-a - by and good- night!

The clumsiness of the word and music accent in this translation at point marked X causes most people to sing the measure in this rhythm.

by   and good

Ex. 89

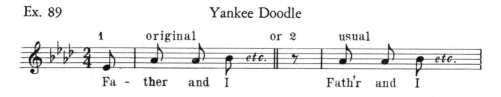

Yankee Doodle

Fa - ther   and   I   Fath'r   and   I

Editors have always been puzzled as to whether to use the original version, No. 1, with its unnatural accent or No. 2 with correct accent but crowded syllables to sing. Neither one is very satisfactory.

RHYMING OF WORDS

Normally, poems that have a pattern of rhyme seem to lend themselves to a musical setting better than poems written in free verse. Because of this, the rhyming dictionary becomes the arranger's best friend when editing the texts of folk songs or in making translations for art songs.

If, however, in an effort to secure a consistent pattern of rhymes, the meaning of the poetry is distorted, or wrong accent of words and music occur, or, unsingable vowels and consonants arise, it is best to relinquish the rhyming pattern momentarily, or, write a smooth text without rhymes. The following poetry, when interpreted correctly, does not rhyme but is so musical and euphonious that it serves as an ideal vehicle for a choral number, especially one in contrapuntal style. In fact, the author came under the spell of its beauty recently and composed a SATB choral number using this poem:*

Ex. 90

A THING OF BEAUTY

A thing of beauty is a joy for ever:
Its loveliness increases; it will never
Pass into nothingness; but still will keep
A bower quiet for us, and a sleep
Full of sweet dreams, and health, and quiet breathing.
from "Endymion"—John Keats

WORDS ON HIGH NOTES

Arrangers unfamiliar with the difficulties which singers have with certain vowels on high notes present added problems in the work of choral directors. In fact, some directors select their music with extreme care with regard to the singable vowels found on extreme high notes. A wise choral arranger will not write high notes using words that contain the vowels, *ee, i,* (especially as in *ing*), *eh,* or *ay* for unchanged treble voices. These vowels must be modified by sopranos from about a top line 'F' on up. Untrained voices who do not understand this literally "choke themselves to death" trying to sing them. On the other hand, the tenors and baritones have little trouble singing these vowels on high notes, in fact, they are often easier than the open vowels of *ah, aw* and *oh*. These latter vowels, especially the *ah,* are the most gracious to treble voices on their high notes. The *oo* vowel is neutral and can be used almost at will, although sopranos need to open it on extreme high notes.

The importance of an easy flow of consonants in the text has been pointed out. This fact is increasingly true in sections of the music which lie high for the part, especially soprano. The difficulty of singing the high section

*"A Thing of Beauty," Carl Fischer, Inc., New York.

of "The Star-Spangled Banner" is well known to all music teachers and directors. The high pitches (when sung in B♭) are only a partial reason for the difficulty. When one examines the unmusical quality of the words, both as to unsingable vowels and consonants of such passages as "The rockets red glare, the bombs bursting in air," the real culprit is evident. It has always been ludicrous to the author that the accepted orchestral arrangement of our National Anthem employs singing strings to express the explosiveness of these words.

EDITING OF TEXTS

Since the choral arranger must fit the words of a folk song or a translation to the music which he is writing, he must be equally adept in editing the texts. It has already been suggested that it is permissible to change an occasional word to secure an easy flow of text; or, to change the rhythmical pattern slightly in various parts to secure a matching of accent with the words.

Some folk songs with a dozen or more verses must be abridged without losing the thread of thought or story. Sometimes, verses need to be combined while others need to be omitted. Occasionally, questionable words need to be changed. In arranging Negro spirituals, the newer practice is to use the regular spelling of words, rather than dialect. The performers can then follow their own preference or discretion as to whether or not to sing the arrangement in dialect. The same practice is followed with most mountain or hillbilly songs.

Words with more than one syllable should be hyphenated to fit the notes, one syllable to a note, such as *moth-er* or *fa-ther*. When in doubt consult the dictionary. A single line, even with the bottom of the word, should be drawn to indicate the number of notes that the word sustains.

It goes without saying that grammatical errors should not occur unless they are typical of a native folk song, in which case it would lose its indigenous character if changed. Care should also be exercised in the punctuation of words in either poetry or prose. The key to phrasing choral music is found in the words and correct punctuation of the text is of untold value to the director in achieving a musical and artistic performance.

CHAPTER X

PREPARING AND SUBMITTING MANUSCRIPTS

The first nine chapters of this book have been committed to the idea that students and choral directors should devote time to making choral arrangements for practical use and, more important still, the growth in musicianship which it will foster in them. The author attributes the greater part of his own musical development to the writing of many choral arrangements and continuous practice of choral composition.

However, every composer or arranger, sooner or later, will have a keen desire to see his name in print. The publication of his creative efforts becomes an ever-increasingly important goal. This desire for recognition and approbation is probably stronger than the anticipation of remunerative reward which is usually rather frugal compared to the amount of time and effort that goes into the writing of choral arrangements. If an arranger is going to write for publication he must first discipline his writing so as to conform with the demand or needs in the field. After he has established a reputation as an arranger, he may then give vent to his own individual creative ideas.

Many amateurs, carried away by stories of fabulous returns from popular songs, try their hand at writing one. There are probably many good unpublished songs floating around the country, but the expense and precariousness of the exploitation of a popular song makes it almost prohibitive for a publisher to take a chance on a novice composer, regardless of the merits of the song. Therefore, he naturally turns to the professional song writer and is reluctant to even look at the songs of amateurs. As suggested earlier, the amateur with ambitions in this area should seek professional collaboration, at first, so as to gain entree to publishers.

Likewise, it is useless for a teacher to make an arrangement of a popular song for his own choral group and, in light of its local success, submit it to the publisher of the song for publication. The fact is that he is breaking the copyright law in making such an arrangement unless he has secured permission from the publisher who owns the copyright. Through correspondence or personal acquaintanceship, he may be able to convince the publisher that he has a unique way of arranging popular songs which would make them very useful to school groups. The publisher then might become sufficiently interested to ask him to "try his hand" at a few and submit them for consideration. On the whole, however, the publishers of popular songs are inclined to turn to their own professional arrangers for publications in the choral field. These arrangers, though highly skilled in various branches of arranging, are not all conversant with the needs of amateur and school choral groups. This is probably the reason for the many popular song arrangements which are not adapted to or usable by school choral groups.

Therefore, it is best for the choral arranger who is bent on the publication of his efforts to turn to the field of the folk song as suggested in Chapter I. Here is a rich field of materials which most publishers, if they are interested at all in choral music, are willing to consider for inclusion in their catalogues. The re-arranging of standard choral works from mixed voices to treble or male voice numbers is also a field which provides an easy and acceptable road to publication.

COPYRIGHT CLEARANCE

Great care must be taken that the words and melody of a song are in public domain (p.d.) before an arranger begins work on a number. In the United States, the copyright of a musical composition or arrangement extends over a period of 28 years. After this period the publisher, the author, or the composer may renew the copyright for another 28 years. Consequently, it is the safest practice to make sure that a song is 56 years old before assuming that it is in public domain and thus free to be arranged.

Of course, this fact immediately eliminates the availability of the present-day popular song (except where permission is granted by the publisher) and leaves only the songs of the gay-nineties and early minstrel songs. Caution must also be exercised in the art song field. The contemporary art song enjoys the same copyright status as the popular song; therefore, the arranger of art songs must turn to the songs of the past century or the canzonettas of an earlier period.

Even the copyright status of folk songs must be established. One would think that anything labeled a 'folk song' would be in public domain, but it is not necessarily so. One collector of folk songs may change and edit a version on which he obtains a copyright and it becomes identified with him. Even though it is not written in voice parts, this version is considered an 'arrangement' and enjoys the same copyright status as an original song. Another collector may come out with a slightly different version of the same song on which he also obtains a copyright. Many arrangers simply make enough changes in a version to avoid copyright infringement.

If the same version of a folk song is published by several different publishers, it is generally safe to assume that this version is in public domain. The usual version of "Home on the Range" is an example. There are some cases where a folk song is in public domain but the arranger has inserted an original (or derivative) middle section which he has copyrighted. The well-known arrangement by David Guion of "Home on the Range" (G. Schirmer) is an example.

Equal care and research must be exercised in the use of texts and translations. The copyright law is as applicable to the words as to the music. In making a translation of an art song, it is always best to go to the original source. Often, the melodies of folk songs are in public domain although the words are copyrighted. Such is the case with some of the Negro spirituals. When in doubt consult the Copyright Office, Library of Congress; American Society of Composers, Authors, and Publishers (ASCAP); or the publisher.

The whole status of the copyright of folk songs needs clarification. As one editor puts it, "If a folk song isn't in public domain, what is?" This is a liberal point of view, for most collectors of folk songs (especially American ones) zealously guard their copyrights. Some of these collectors have a flat fee, usually $10.00, for the permission to make a choral arrangement of one of the folk songs from their collections. It seems that the privilege of labelling anything a 'folk song' should carry with it the responsibility of indicating what is 'folk' and what is 'individual'; or, in other words, what is public domain and what can be copyrighted.

The Business Handbook of Music Education, a manual published by the Music Education Exhibitors Association, an auxiliary of the Music Educators National Conference (MENC) clearly explains the copyright law in the following quotation from this valuable little book. It is addressed to the music teacher but is equally informative to the arranger and composer. An extended and annotated list of publishers which provides the arranger with active outlets to whom he can submit his wares is also included in the book. Copies of this handbook may be secured, free of charge, from the Music Education Exhibitors Association, 64 East Jackson Blvd., Suite 804, Chicago 4, Illinois.

THE COPYRIGHT LAW

Some instructors have gained the mistaken impression that copying of copyrighted material is permissible and legal as long as the copied material is not sold for profit.

Composers and publishers invest their talent, efforts, and capital in publications. They are entitled to the income from the sale of these items. Any practice of copying which deprives the composer and publisher of just and deserved royalties and sales is an unfair practice and is definitely a violation of the copyright law of the United States of America.

Following are phrases taken directly from the copyright laws:

. . . any person entitled thereto, (the person securing the copyright) . . . *shall have the exclusive right* (a) to print, reprint, publish, copy, and vend the copyrighted work; (b) to arrange or adapt it if it be a musical work; (c) to make or to procure the making of any transcription or record by or from which . . . it may in any manner or by any method be exhibited, performed, represented, produced, or reproduced; (d) to perform the copyrighted work publicly for profit if it be a musical composition; (e) to make any arrangement or setting of it or of the melody of it in any system of notation.

That any person who willfully and for profit shall infringe any copyright secured by this Act, or who shall knowingly and willfully aid or abet such infringement, shall be deemed guilty of a misdemeanor, and upon conviction thereof shall be punished by imprisonment for not exceeding one year or by a fine of not less than one hundred dollars nor more than one thousand dollars, or both, in the discretion of the court.

Following is a copy of a statement issued by the Standard Music Publishers' Association of the United States:

Unauthorized Copying of Copyrighted Material Illegal!

Copying by any process — by hand on paper or blackboard, by multigraphing, mimeographing, photostating or any other method — of any part of a copyrighted work, no matter for what purpose or use (religious, educational, theatrical or otherwise), without the permission of the copyright owner, is a serious offense against the United States law, punishable with heavy fines beginning at one hundred dollars, plus minimum damages of two hundred and fifty dollars. The United States copyright laws are very strict in this particular and many actions are now being conducted against teachers, directors and other offenders making unauthorized arrangements or copies. The practice is unfair to composers, authors and publishers.

The law is specific and clear. *In spirit and fact you are guilty of infringement if in any case you through act or sanction, without express permission of the copyright owners, do any of the following:*

(1) Reproduce copyrighted words or music through the use of mimeograph stencils.

(2) Make a song slide of a copyrighted song.

(3) Write the words or music of such a song on the blackboard.

(4) Copy extra parts for your band or orchestra.

(5) Make any arrangement of copyrighted music.

If you are in doubt as to what *is* "copyrighted music" we would point out that the United States Copyright Law requires that notice of copyright ownership, showing the name of the owner and the year of copyright, be printed on all copies of a copyrighted work. Therefore, when such notice appears, it is definite evidence that permission for copying must be secured from the copyright owner *before* it may be copied.

To avoid the hazard of infringement, check carefully the copyright ownership as shown in this notice, and first obtain the desired permission or *leave it alone!*

In the case of materials published outside the United States, the laws require no specific notice of copyright, and inquiry as to copyright status should therefore be made of the publisher or his American representative.

MARKET FOR ARRANGEMENTS

The so-called renaissance of choral music in this country in the past 25 years has opened a rich market for choral music. Never before have music publishers, both popular and standard, been so eager to obtain choral compositions and arrangements suitable for school, church, and amateur choirs. Many publishers are devoting the greater part of their efforts to the publication of appropriate choral music. Therefore, if an arranger can feel the pulse of the choral needs of these amateur choirs and can write music accordingly, there is a waiting market for his wares.

CONSIDERATION OF MANUSCRIPTS

The reluctance of many publishers to consider manuscripts of unknown arrangers and composers, especially in the popular field, has already been mentioned. Nevertheless, it is true that most publishers will consider manuscripts which seem to fill a style needed in their catalogues. (As mentioned before, arrangements and compositions for three-part treble voice groups are always in demand.)

It is probably best to submit the arrangement to a publisher's representative with whom he may be acquainted, preferably one in the education department. This representative may personally send it to the editorial department; or, he may give the arranger permission to use his name when submitting it himself to the publisher. This personal touch may or may not do any good (especially if it is a bad arrangement) but it can't hurt. If the number has had performances and has been included on printed programs, it is well to send these along with the manuscript. Naturally, publishers will show more interest in an arranger's manuscripts if the arranger is in a position to help exploit the music by obtaining performances of it or aranging for its use by school and amateur groups. Nevertheless, regardless of personal contact or professional prestige, the secret of securing consideration of one's manuscripts is the ability to turn out good material that is needed in the field.

SUBMITTING OF MANUSCRIPTS

In submitting manuscripts an arranger should be careful that they are neat and correct. If an author submitted a book to a publisher with words mispelled, grammatical mistakes, and wrong punctuation, the publisher could hardly be expected to review it in a favorable light. When a music publisher receives a manuscript written sloppily and filled with mistakes, he naturally assumes that the arranger doesn't know his business and gives it little consideration.

The manuscript should be written in ink on large, 12 stave, manuscript paper of individual four page sheets. A very clear pencil copy (Use a No. 1 pencil) is also acceptable. The writing should be spread evenly so as not to appear crowded or cramped. (Don't be stingy with manuscript paper.) The words should be printed clearly or typed in under each voice part.

The *tempo* and expression marks may be written in Italian or English. It is most logical to make it a practice to use *either* the Italian or the English terms consistently throughout the arrangement, never to mix the two. Except for *tempo* marks at the beginning, which should appear above the top voice part and piano part, all other expression marks should be written in each part as follows:

Ex. 91

CORRECT NOTATION

All arrangers should be acquainted with the established practices of music notation. Turning in correctly edited manuscripts is important.

General rules for the mechanics of notation:

    1. Time signatures follow the key signatures on the staff.

        Time signatures are used only at the beginning of the music and at each change of meter.

        Key signatures are used on each staff throughout the piece.

Ex. 92

    2. Stems turn up wnen note-head is below the third line.

Ex. 93

    3. Stems turn down when note-head is above the third line.

Ex. 94

    4. Stems turn up or down when note-head is on the third line.

        Many editors always turn the stem down; others follow the practice of keeping a symmetry with the general pattern.

Ex. 95

    5. When several stems are joined together the stems turn up or down determined by the majority or general position of the note-heads.

Ex. 96

6. When more than one voice part appears on a staff, all stems turn up
   for the higher part and down for the lower part.

   When both parts sing the same note, stems turn both up and down.

Ex. 97

7. The indication for triplets is written near the note-heads, (not the
   stems).

Ex. 98

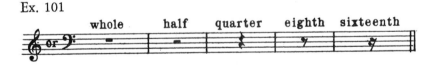

8. The dot after a note is always placed in a space, (not on a line).

Ex. 99

9. A dot after a note-head on a line is placed slightly above the line.

Ex. 100

10. Rests are placed in the middle of the staff when there is only one voice
    part, whole rests and half rests being written in the third space.

Ex. 101

11. The positions of rests vary when two or more voice parts are written
    on a staff. (A whole rest is used to indicate a full measure regardless
    of the number of beats.)

Ex. 102

12. The flags of eighth and sixteenth notes are always placed on the right side of the stem, unless stems are connected, then they are placed on the inside.

Ex. 103

13. The tie or slur is usually written near the note-heads. However, in engraving, the slur may be placed next to the flag of connected notes to save space.

Ex. 104

14. First and second endings are notated as follows:

In choral music it is best to write out repeats rather than indicate them when words are different for each repetition, unless the length of the number makes it prohibitive in terms of costs.

Ex. 105

15. No repeat marks are necessary to accompany the *Da Capo* (D.C.), (back to the beginning); or *Dal Segno* (D.S.), (back to the sign).

16. In notating syncopated rhythms extreme care must be taken that each beat of the measure is clear.

Ex. 106

17. In voice parts, stems are separated for each syllable but in piano parts they are connected. Stems are connected in voice parts when several notes are used with one syllable.

Ex. 107

TUTU MARAMBA★

Chorus for Mixed Voices A Cappella
S.A.T.B.B.

Translation by
H. R. W.

BRAZILIAN FOLK SONG
Arr. by H. R. W.

★Pronounced Too-Too Mah-rahm-bah

Copyright 1942 by Hall & McCreary Company, Chicago   Octavo No. 1088
(Used by Permission)

18. In octavo music when the piano part is a duplication of the voice parts, stems are separated in voice parts and connected in piano parts.

Ex. 108

AT PARTING
T.T.B.B.

FREDERIC PETERSON

HARRY R. WILSON

The fra-grance it ex - hales, __ Ah! if you on - ly knew! __

19. When one piano staff serves for both voices and piano, (as in hymn books and song books) the notes of each staff are written on the same stem, its direction depending upon the position of the note-heads, except in unisons, seconds, and cross rhythms.

Ex. 109

NOW THE DAY IS OVER

SABINE BARING GOULD

JOSEPH BARNBY

Now the day is o - ver, Night is draw - ing nigh; __

Shad - ows of the eve - ning Steal a-cross the sky. A - men.

20. The direction of the stems in piano accompaniments are illustrated in the following two examples. Notice, that in Ex. 110, the stems of the melody turn up regardless of the position of the notes, while the stems of the afterbeats turn down, except when the melody is below the afterbeats as in Measure 4. In Ex. 111, the stems of the bass notes turn up while the stems of the afterbeats turn down.

Ex. 110

From the "GRAND CANYON SUITE"
ON THE TRAIL
Four Part S.A.T.B.

Lyric by
HAROLD ADAMSON

Music by
FERDE GROFE

Ex. 111

K - K - K - KATY
Four Part S.A.T.B.

by
GEOFFREY O'HARA

21. When employing enharmonic changes of notation to avoid the use of double flats or double sharps, the shift of key should be made gracefully, usually at the beginning of a bar, rather than within the bar. The following example illustrates the use of enharmonic notation.

Ex. 112

THE SONG OF THE SWAMPS
BARITONE SOLO
(S.A.T.B.)

Lyric by
FLORENCE TARR

Music by
HARRY ROBERT WILSON

CONCLUSION

More details of the practices in editing music can be learned by studying representative publications. Of course, the editors and proof-readers are responsible for the correctness of the published copy. However, there is a better chance to have the published copy perfect if the composer or arranger turns in a carefully edited manuscript with as few mistakes as possible. This would obviate the necessity for making changes on engraved plates, which is a very costly operation.

As a parting paragraph, to give a word of encouragement to amateur arrangers who are endeavouring to break into the publication field. Don't ever give up. Don't submit a book full of manuscripts — rather select a few of the best and send them in, or, better yet, concentrate on one if it is something a little unusual. The first step is to have faith in your own work! Creative talent of professional calibre in the choral field is limited and there is always an opportunity for those who persevere! Good luck!